Questions & Answers
about
DEPRESSION
and Its
Treatment

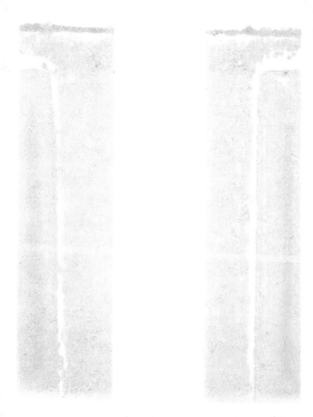

Questions & Answers
about
DEPRESSION
and Its
Treatment

A CONSULTATION WITH
A LEADING
PSYCHIATRIST

Ivan K. Goldberg, MD

The Charles Press, Publishers
Philadelphia

Copyright ©1993 by The Charles Press, Publishers, Inc.

All rights reserved.

This book, or any parts thereof, may not be used or reproduced in any manner without written permission of The Charles Press.

The Charles Press, Publishers
Post Office Box 15715
Philadelphia, PA 19103

Library of Congress Cataloging-in-Publication Data

Goldberg, Ivan, K., 1934-
   Questions and answers about depression and its treatment: a
   consultation with a leading psychiatrist / Ivan K. Goldberg.
       p.   cm.

   Includes bibliographical references.
   ISBN 0-914783-68-8
   1.Depression, Mental — Miscellanea. 2.Affective disorders—
   Miscellanea.   I. Title.
   RC537.G655   1993
   616.85'27—dc20   93-9430
                                                                        CIP

ISBN 0-914783-68-8

Printed in the United States of America

68737

Foreword

Here is a book that cried out to be written; it is surprising that no one thought of it before. How fortunate that the one who did think of it is Dr. Ivan Goldberg. He is a specialist in psychiatry who focuses on depression and mood disorders. In addition to his excellent academic credentials, Dr. Goldberg is a compassionate psychiatrist who knows how to listen and talk with patients and their families.

Why is Dr. Goldberg's book so important and valuable? After all, don't we go to doctors and expect them to take good care of us? Why do we have to ask questions? Isn't it true that "The doctor knows best—just do as I say and everything will be well"? Not any longer. Today's patients want and deserve to be full partners in their treatment. They want to be well informed. Physicians who are doing their job well will encourage patients to learn as much as they can about their illness and its treatment. Good physicians will spend as much time as possible providing information to their patients.

Unfortunately, doctors often do not have as much time to talk with patients as they would like. And here is where Dr. Goldberg's book comes in. *Questions and Answers About Depression and Its Treatment* is based on Ivan Goldberg's solid knowledge and extensive experience in treating depressed patients. It differs from most books on this subject found in bookstores in that the author is truly an expert in his field; from his direct contact with hundreds of depressed people he knows what they want to know about the many aspects of diagnosis and treatment. Dr. Goldberg writes in a way that is easy for a non-professional to read and understand. It is as if you were having a personal consultation with Dr. Goldberg or were attending one of his lectures. Among the special features that make this such a useful book are that it is full of information not available in any other single source and that its concepts and treatments are up-to-the-minute. For example, Dr. Goldberg explains to patients how the recently enacted Americans with Disabilities Act protects them if their job is jeopardized by their mood disorder or by the side effects of medications.

If you or a member of your family are suffering from depression or manic depression—or if you think you or they might be—read this book. If you are already in treatment, ask your therapist to read *Questions and Answers About Depression and Its Treatment*. I am sure your therapist will agree. Indeed, I intend to advise my own patients and the young physicians I help train to be psychiatrists to read this excellent book. Thank you, Ivan Goldberg.

R.V. Fitzgerald, MD
Clinical Professor
Department of Psychiatry
Medical College of Ohio at Toledo

Preface

As a consultant psychiatrist who sees many patients referred by other physicians and mental health professionals, I am repeatedly impressed by the number of searching, intelligent questions that patients ask me regarding depression and its treatment. Clearly, today's patients want to participate in decisions about their care—as well they should— and to do so they seek more and more information about their particular problems. This book is meant as a step in that direction.

Specifically, the objective of this book is to make available, in easily understood form and language, the answers to the most frequently asked questions about depression and related mood disorders (including manic depression). Many of these questions have been posed by patients, their families, referring physicians, psychiatric nurses, social workers and psychotherapists. Other questions have been asked of me while lecturing, particularly from individuals who are members of various mood disorder support groups.

I have categorized the questions and answers according to subject matter. In selecting the questions, I have attempted to present a reasonably complete picture of depression and manic depression, ranging from symptoms and diagnostic methods to suicide and legal issues. However, the number of questions on a particular subject is related to the relative frequency with which these questions have been asked. Consequently, the largest section of the book concerns methods of treatment, including degree of effectiveness, side effects and precautions.

It is only fair for the reader to ask about the validity and soundness of my answers, especially in the event that others may disagree. The answers are based on my own extensive experience as a psychiatrist specializing in depression and manic depression. I also serve as director of the New York Psychopharmacologic Institute and have been on the faculty of the Department of Psychiatry at Columbia University's College of Physicians and Surgeons for over 30 years. Above all, the answers have been read by several of my esteemed colleagues, who suggested a number of pertinent changes.

I can only hope that *Questions and Answers About Depression and Its Treatment* will clarify many aspects of the subject for patients and their families, as well as for mental health professionals in every care setting.

Ivan K. Goldberg, MD

Acknowledgments

I would like to express my gratitude to the members of various mood disorders support groups (MDSGs) who have invited me to their meetings to answer their questions about depression and manic depression. Many of the questions in this book originate from questions I have been asked at these meetings.

I am indebted to my colleagues and friends who have contributed to this book by reading one or more sections of the manuscript. Their pointed comments and criticisms have helped me sharpen my thinking regarding mood disorders and their treatment. For their helpful comments in many areas, I extend my heartfelt gratitude to David Chowes, Harold B. Esecover, MD, R. Vance Fitzgerald and David G. Zick, MD. For the past 7 years, the members of PsyComNet have contributed a great deal to my understanding of the treatment of mood disorders. I am especially thankful for the help I have received from the librarians of the New York State Psychiatric Institute, the College of Physicians and Surgeons of Columbia University, the New York Academy of Medicine and the National Library of Medicine in Bethesda, Maryland. Their assistance was well above and beyond the call of duty.

Special thanks to my daughters, Meredith Goldberg and Bonni Goldberg, for their patience during the time I was preoccupied with preparing the manuscript of this book.

I.K.G.

Contents

SECTION 3: SPECIAL ASPECTS OF MOOD DISORDERS

Questions & Answers
about
DEPRESSION
and Its
Treatment

SECTION 1

An Introduction to Depression and Mood Disorders

DEFINITIONS

Q: How do I know if I am depressed or if I am just sad or blue?

A: A depression is a persistent period of an excessively low, sad, blue mood that is severe enough to interfere with a major life activity such as work, school, family responsibilities and inter-personal relationships. Depression often leads to changes in self-esteem, concentration and sleep and appetite, while feelings of sadness usually do not cause these symptoms. When people are depressed they often lack interest in and do not derive pleasure from usually satisfying activities, but this does not generally happen when someone is simply sad.

Q: When I am depressed I have the feeling that I am more dead than alive. The whole world seems to be in black and white rather than in color. Are these feelings typical of depression?

A: When you are depressed it is not unusual to have these types of feelings. I have heard people who are depressed say that they feel as if they are in a very heavy fog — as if their body is heavy and hard to move. They also say that they feel totally hopeless and useless.

Q: What is manic depression?

A: Manic depression, now called bipolar disorder, is a mood disorder in which a person experiences both very high moods (called manic episodes) and moods of severe depression.

Q: What is a manic episode?

A: A manic episode is a period of overactivity accompanied by several of the following symptoms: elevated or irritable mood, overtalkativeness, inflated self-esteem, decreased need for sleep, distractibility, poor judgment, impulsivity and, at times, psychotic behavior. Because of poor judgment and impulsive behavior, when a person is in a manic episode he often becomes involved in activities that may result in harm, such as foolish sexual encounters, excessive buying sprees, driving much too fast and making dubious investments. It is difficult to convince people who are in a manic episode to consult a physician because they often feel that there is nothing wrong with them. They often also believe that they know more about themselves than a doctor would.

Q: My doctor tells me that when I come out of a depression I go through a brief period of hypomania. What is the difference between mania and hypomania?

A: Hypomania is similar to mania, but it is less severe. Those who are hypomanic generally feel physically well, have more energy than usual and a have a decreased need for sleep. They also show an increase in the speed and quantity of physical and mental activities, are more sociable and talkative than usual, and they think more easily and creatively than they do when they are depressed. They often have a better sense of self-esteem and are more talkative than usual. They may also be unusually restless and impulsive. In addition, they may joke and laugh a lot. Their increased levels of activity and talkativeness can be so excessive that it is annoying to those around them. Unlike those in a manic state, people who are hypomanic do not experience a complete disruption of social and work activities. Some people who become hypomanic never become manic, while others have episodes of both hypomania and mania. It is rare for persons to recognize that they are hypomanic; when asked how they feel, people who are hypomanic will usually reply that they are fine and that they do not feel at all "hyped-up" (manic).

Q: I have been diagnosed as Bipolar II. What does this mean?

A: People with bipolar disorder are divided into two groups—Bipolar I and Bipolar II. Those designated as Bipolar I sequentially experience episodes of both severe depression and manic periods. The diagnosis Bipolar II is given to people who have severe depressions, but who experience episodes of hypomania, not mania. (Those diagnosed as Bipolar II will often respond to a combination of lithium and Prozac if they have failed to respond to other antidepressants.)

Q: What is cyclothymia?

A: Cyclothymia is the mildest form of bipolar mood disorder. Usually developing early in adult life, cyclothymia is characterized by many periods of both mild elation and depression. Those with cyclothymia may experience many months of normal moods; their mood swings are spontaneous and are not reactions to life events. Cyclothymia is often seen in relatives of those with bipolar disorder and some people with cyclothymia will go on to develop bipolar disorder.

Q: What is dysthymia?

A: Dysthymia is a state of relatively mild chronic depression that usually lasts for over 2 years. There is probably more than one kind of dysthymia. People with dysthymia experience depression, changes in appetite and sleep, hopeless thoughts, problems with decision-making, poor concentration, lack of energy, fatigue and poor self-esteem. Dysthymia often starts early in life—in the teens or early 20s. Some people date the onset of their dysthymia back to early childhood and feel that they were probably "born depressed." Dysthymia may also develop in older adults, particularly following a severe depression, a bereavement or other major stress. Dysthymia is often accompanied by social aloofness, lack of assertiveness and periods of more severe depression. While psychotherapy helps some people with dysthymia, antidepressant therapy is often especially effective in those dysthymic people whose relatives had (or have) severe mood disorders. It has been estimated that about 3 percent of the population of the United States has dysthymia.

Q: My psychiatrist says that I have double depression. What is this and what can I do about it?

A: Double depression is when someone with dysthymia also has episodes of more severe depression. When the more severe depressive spells remit, the person goes back into a state of dysthymia. Antidepressant therapy often helps both the dysthymia and the periods of more severe depression.

Q: My doctor says that I have an atypical depression. What is an atypical depression and how does it differ from other forms of depression?

A: Atypical depression is a form of depression in which a depressed mood can be at least temporarily improved by good news or by other pleasurable experiences. This is in contrast to the fixed depressed mood characteristic of other types of depression. People with atypical depression may oversleep, overeat and feel as if their bodies are heavy and difficult to move. Compared to people with other types of depressions, those with atypical depression often feel better in the morning and become increasingly depressed as the day progresses. Those with atypical depression usually do not have the energy or interest to seek or arrange pleasurable experiences. Their capacity to enjoy pleasure is intact and if a pleasurable situation presents itself, they can enjoy it. With other types of depression people may experience the inability to both seek pleasure and experience pleasure. Despite its name, atypical depression is not a rare condition.

Q: I am a teacher. Some of my colleagues have stopped teaching because they claim that they are "burned out." Is burn-out the same as depression?

A: Many people are unwilling (or unable) to recognize the true nature of their problem. Claiming that they are experiencing burn-out is one way that people try to explain their depression. The psychotherapeutic approaches that are effective for the treatment of those with depression are similarly effective for people who feel that they are burned out. If the depressive symptoms experienced are severe or there is no improvement following 6 months of psychotherapy, it would be worthwhile to pursue psychopharmacologic treatment.

Q: What is the difference between unipolar and bipolar depression?

A: A unipolar depression is never associated with periods of mania. In bipolar depression, there are periods of both depression and mania.

Q: I have had manic periods a few times, but I've never felt depressed. Does this mean that I have unipolar or bipolar depression?

A: Confusing as this sounds, people who only have manic episodes are considered bipolar. There are some individuals who may remain in a manic episode for years without ever becoming depressed.

Q: Are serious mood disorders considered physical or emotional illnesses?

A: While it used to be believed that emotional factors were the main cause of mood disorders, the importance of biological (i.e., chemical) changes in the brain have recently been recognized. People with mood disorders have alterations in brain chemistry that are probably responsible for the intensity of their depressed or manic feelings. For example, researchers have recently discovered that the brain cells of depressed people metabolize less glucose than the brain cells of non-depressed people. Emotional factors, thinking patterns, stress and life styles also contribute to the onset and subsequent course of mood disorders. In other words, both chemical and emotional factors can produce mood disorders.

Q: When I talk to my family about the way that I feel both de-
        pressed and high at the same time, they say that this is impossi-
        ble. How might I better explain what I am experiencing so they
        will understand my problem?

A: People often mistakenly believe that manic, normal and depressed
        moods are arranged on a vertical line with mania being at the high
        end, normal mood in the middle and depression at the low end. A
        more useful way of understanding the situation is as a triangle with
        normal mood at one angle, mania at the second angle and depres-
        sion at the third. You can draw a triangle and use it to explain that
        your moods may be at a point within the triangle that is far from
        normal yet also both depressed and manic. Individuals who have
        manic and depressive symptoms simultaneously are referred to as
        being in a mixed state. Mixed states are common and are extremely
        uncomfortable. Unfortunately, they are often overlooked by men-
        tal health professionals.

Q: I have episodes of depression at least once every couple of
        months. Is this frequency normal?

A: For bipolar patients, the time between one episode of mania or
        depression and the onset of the next is usually many months.
        However, almost one in five bipolar patients has four or more
        episodes of mania or depression each year. This condition is
        called rapid cycling. Rapid cycling occurs more often in women
        than men. This may result, at least partially, from hypothyroid-
        ism, which is much more common in women. Some people with
        unipolar depression (depression without mania) also rapidly
        cycle between normal and depressed moods. Such people actu-
        ally may be bipolar, and lithium is an effective treatment for
        depressed people showing such a pattern.

Q: I have had two episodes of depression. I am now 32 and preg-
        nant for the first time. Is it likely that I will become depressed
        after the birth of my child?

A: Depressions after childbirth, called postpartum depressions,
        range in severity from the occurrence of a period of mild blues
        a few days after delivery, which approximately three-quarters
        of new mothers experience, to severe, incapacitating depres-

sions that affect up to 10 percent of mothers in the postpartum period. The rapid hormonal changes that occur around the time of childbirth may trigger some women's vulnerability to depression. Some women only have depressions following childbirth and are then depression-free for the remainder of their lives. Women who have had episodes of depression before pregnancy are more at risk for experiencing postpartum depression than women who have never been depressed. However, it is reassuring to know that most women with a history of depression do not have a severe depression following childbirth. Women who develop severe postpartum depression should have prompt treatment; this depression can last for months and interfere with mother-infant bonding. Severe postpartum depression, like other depressions, usually responds best to a combined treatment that includes psychotherapy and antidepressant medication.

Q: I get depressed each fall and winter. What causes this pattern?

A: It has been discovered that the amount of light people are exposed to affects the way they feel. People with this disorder, called seasonal affective disorder (SAD), typically become depressed in the fall or winter and remain depressed until spring when the days become longer. Both antidepressants and exposure to bright light effectively treat SAD. Although light boxes are sold for the treatment of SAD, taking a 30-minute walk outside every day when it is bright enough to see your shadow will also have a therapeutic effect. There is also a rare form of SAD in which people become depressed in the summer. If they wear dark sunglasses throughout the day they will become less depressed.

Q: What is schizoaffective disorder?

A: This is a condition in which there is a mixture of the symptoms of schizophrenia and mood disorders. Patients with schizoaffective disorder may have manic and/or depressed symptoms along with hallucinations and bizarre delusions. It is often difficult to tell schizoaffective disorder from the psychotic forms of mania or depression.

Q: I have been depressed a few times and every time this happens I am afraid I am going crazy. Will my depressions cause me to become insane?

A: No. Many people fear that depression will cause them to become permanently out of control, but depression is a highly treatable disorder that does not lead to permanent loss of control.

Q: What are psychotic depressions?

A: Psychotic depressions are severe depressions accompanied by delusions and/or hallucinations. Delusions are fixed false beliefs that cannot be changed by argument. Typical depressive delusions are that recovery is impossible, that the patient's family would be better off if the patient died and that the individual is fatally ill. Hallucinations are false perceptions, such as hearing voices or seeing people who are dead. Those with psychotic depression may respond to treatment with medications or they may respond only to electroconvulsive therapy (ECT).

Q: I have been diagnosed as having major depression. I also have panic attacks. Are the panic attacks a part of my mood disorder or are they a separate problem?

A: People frequently are bothered by both depression and panic attacks. Some of those with depression only have panic attacks when they are severely depressed. Others may have panic attacks at certain times and suffer from depression at other times. Antidepressants are among the most effective treatments for panic attacks. This suggests that as far as brain chemistry goes, there are parallel neurochemical disturbances in panic attacks and depression.

SYMPTOMS AND DIAGNOSIS

Q: Specifically, what are the common symptoms of depression?

A: Some of the symptoms of depression follow:

- Reduced interest in activities
- Indecisiveness
- Feeling sad/blue/unhappy
- Irritability
- Getting too little or too much sleep
- Loss of concentration
- Increased or decreased appetite
- Loss of self-esteem
- Decreased sexual desire
- Problems with memory
- Despair and hopelessness
- Suicidal thoughts
- Reduced pleasurable feelings
- Guilt feelings
- Crying and tearfulness
- Feeling helpless
- Restlessness
- Feeling disorganized
- Difficulty doing things
- Lack of energy and feeling tired
- Self-critical thoughts
- Moving and thinking slowly
- Feeling in a fog or stupor
- Slow speech
- Emotional and physical pain
- Hypochondriacal fears
- Feeling dead
- Delusions of poverty or guilt
- Hallucinations

Q: What are the common symptoms of mania?

A: Roughly in order of increasing severity, the common symptoms are:

- Decreased need for sleep
- Restlessness
- Feeling full of energy
- Distractibility
- Increased talkativeness
- Creative thinking
- Increase in activities
- Feeling elated
- Inappropriate laughing
- Inappropriate humor
- Speeded-up thinking
- Rapid, pressured speech
- Impaired judgment
- Increased religiosity
- Feelings of exhilaration
- Racing thoughts
- Irritability
- Excitability
- Inappropriate behaviors
- Impulsive behavior
- Increased sexuality
- Inflated self-esteem
- Financial extravagance
- Grandiose thinking
- Feelings of omnipotence
- Heightened perceptions
- Bizarre hallucinations
- Disorientation
- Disjointed thinking
- Incoherent speech

- Paranoid thoughts/delu-
  sions
- Hostility/violence
- Frenetic activity
- Severe or total insomnia

- Profound loss of weight
- Catatonia
- Exhaustion/collapse
- Coma/death

Q: Are mood disorders usually accurately diagnosed?

A: Actually, people with depression are frequently misdiagnosed.
Many nonpsychiatric physicians fail to recognize the true nature
of the problem when patients come to them complaining of
subtle symptoms such as insomnia or fatigue. Psychologists and
other non-medical mental health professionals often interpret
the symptoms of depression as resulting from "personality
problems," and fail to refer their patients for appropriate antidepressant therapy. Some psychiatrists tend to diagnose schizophrenia, when the patient is clearly suffering from a psychotic
form of mania or depression. Since about three-quarters of those
suffering from bipolar disorder deny that they have ever had
periods of elevated mood, they are incorrectly diagnosed as
having unipolar depressions.

Q: Which is more common, unipolar or bipolar forms of depression?

A: About one-third of depressed people are diagnosed as having
bipolar disorder, but experts believe that about one-half of all
depressed people are actually bipolar. When giving their history
to a psychiatrist, many neglect to report any hypomanic episodes that they may have had in the past. Frequently a bipolar
individual will have a day or two of hypomania when recovering from a depression. When these or other brief hypomanic
episodes are not reported, the patient may be diagnosed erron-
eously as having a unipolar rather than a bipolar depression.
The likelihood of correct diagnosis increases when an experienced mental health professional takes a history from both the
patient and members of the patient's family.

Q: Can depression cause pain or other physical symptoms?

A: Sometimes people are not aware that they are depressed and do
not understand why they are experiencing various physical

symptoms. They are said to have masked depression. When these patients see a physician they usually do not mention the possibility that they might be depressed, and it takes a skillful physician to diagnose the true situation. The following are some physical symptoms that may accompany depression:

- Headache
- Backache
- Dizziness
- Abdominal pain
- Constipation
- Mouth pain
- Vomiting
- Pins-and-needles
- Palpitations
- Clumsiness
- Pain in the limbs
- Chest pain
- Blurred vision
- Frequent urination
- Insomnia
- Loss of appetite or weight
- Memory problems
- Decreased sexual desire
- Low energy or fatigue
- Decreased sexual performance

Q: Are there any blood or other medical tests that can diagnose depression?

A: There are several tests that have been proposed as methods to improve the accuracy of the diagnosis of depression. Among these tests are the dexamethasone suppression test, a test of the brain system that regulates thyroid function; the measurement of the amount of the chemical MHPG in the urine; and the determination of the length of time between the onset of sleep and the start of the first dream of the night. While these tests are useful as research techniques, none of them has shown an ability to differentiate depressed and nondepressed people with sufficient accuracy to become the "gold standard" by which depression can be diagnosed. Psychiatrists sometimes resort to these tests when there is some doubt about an individual's diagnosis.

Q: Are the symptoms of depression the same in unipolar and bipolar patients?

A: There are some depressive symptoms that are especially likely to be found in bipolar patients. While unipolar patients often complain of insomnia and loss of weight, bipolar patients frequently show a pattern of oversleeping and overeating when depressed. Profound fatigue, the inability to make oneself do things and slowing of mental processes and physical movements are especially likely to be found in depressed bipolar patients. Those who show this pattern often demonstrate the best response treatment with a monoamine oxidase (MAO) inhibitor combined with lithium.

Q: I have been depressed many times but I have never been hypomanic or manic. Because I have frequent depressive episodes and oversleep when I am depressed, my psychiatrist says that I may be bipolar. Would it make sense for me to be treated as if I am bipolar even though I have never had a manic episode?

A: As mentioned earlier, there are many people who appear to have unipolar depressions without manic episodes, but who in fact have bipolar disorder. These individuals may often be recognized by the early age at which they first became depressed, by a family history that includes one or more bipolar relatives, by frequent episodes of depression and by a tendency to oversleep and overeat when depressed. Depressed people who show such characteristics often respond very well to lithium by itself or to lithium combined with an antidepressant.

Q: During three severe manic episodes I have heard voices. Does that mean that I am schizophrenic?

A: Hallucinations (false perceptions) and delusions (fixed false beliefs) are psychotic symptoms that sometimes occur during severe manic episodes. The diagnosis in such instances is mania with psychosis, not schizophrenia.

Q: I have had many periods of severe depression and two very mild periods of hypomania. Does that mean I am unipolar or bipolar?

A: The occurrence of one manic or hypomanic episode in someone with a history of depression is all that is needed to make the diagnosis of a bipolar disorder.

Q: What are the common themes of hallucinations and delusions in mania?

A: The most common themes are the beliefs that people have special insights or powers concerning religion, politics, sex, business and finance, or the belief that they are being persecuted in some manner.

Q: Some years ago I was diagnosed as schizophrenic and was subsequently hospitalized twice for acute psychotic episodes. Recently, when I became severely depressed, my diagnosis was changed to bipolar disorder. Why didn't the doctors recognize that I was having manic episodes?

A: For many years, psychiatrists, especially in the United States, considered that almost all psychotic patients were suffering from schizophrenia of one form or another. Only recently has it been recognized that many patients who were previously diagnosed as schizophrenic were suffering from a manic episode with psychotic features.

Q: Are there differences in depression in blacks and whites?

A: There has not been much epidemiological data gathered regarding the prevalence of depression in blacks compared to whites. One study of Asian, hispanic, black and white adolescents showed no significant differences in the frequency of depression in the respective groups. A study of depressed black and white adults found that there was a higher rate of suicide threats and attempts among black males than among white males.

Q: Have depressive symptoms changed over the years?

A: The symptoms of depression have not changed in over 2000 years. Then, as now, depressed people had low self-esteem, gloomy thoughts about the future, problems with concentration, disturbances in sleep and appetite, feelings of unworthiness and thoughts of self-destruction. Depression and suicide are reported in ancient Greek, Latin and Hebrew texts.

WHO GETS MOOD DISORDERS?

Q: How common is depression in the United States?

A: At any given moment, there are probably about 12 million Americans who are depressed. The vast majority of these depressed individuals are not receiving any sort of treatment for their problems because neither they themselves, nor their physicians or relatives realize that they are depressed. A man has about a 10 percent chance of becoming depressed at some point in his lifetime and a woman has about a 23 percent chance. Another way of looking at this is to consider that each year about 5 percent of the population will experience a mood disorder of sufficient severity to justify psychiatric treatment. The risk of developing bipolar illness is approximately 1 percent in both men and women.

Q: Is it true that married people are less likely to become depressed than single people?

A: Studies have shown that the incidence of depression is higher in single, divorced and separated persons than it is among those who are married. From greatest to least, the order is as follows:

- Separated and divorced women
- Single, widowed and divorced men
- Single and widowed women
- Married women
- Married men

Q: Do mood disorders develop mostly among "losers"?

A: By no means. Many very successful men and women have suffered from mood disorders. Authorities believe that the following well-known people have been afflicted:

- Diane Arbus
- Honore de Balzac
- Ludwig van Beethoven
- Hector Berlioz
- John Berryman
- William Blake
- Lord Byron
- Winston Churchill

- Samuel Coleridge
- Oliver Cromwell
- Claude Debussy
- Charles Dickens
- Ralph Waldo Emerson
- George Fox
- Johann Wolfgang von Goethe
- Alexander Hamilton
- Ernest Hemingway
- George Frederick Handel
- John Keats
- Robert E. Lee
- Abraham Lincoln
- Robert Lowell
- Martin Luther
- Gustav Mahler
- John Stuart Mill
- Wolfgang Amadeus Mozart
- Benito Mussolini
- Friedrich Nietzsche
- Gen. George S. Patton
- Sylvia Plath
- Edgar Allan Poe
- Ezra Pound
- Jackson Pollock
- Theodore Roethke
- Theodore Roosevelt
- Gioacchino Rossini
- Mark Rothko
- John Ruskin
- Robert Schumann
- Anne Sexton
- Percy Shelley
- William Styron
- Emmanual Swedenborg
- Vincent Van Gogh
- Virginia Woolf

Q: Is it true that writers are especially likely to have bipolar disorder?

A: Apparently so. A study found that more writers, including many famous ones, had bipolar disorders more often than the rest of the general population.

COURSE AND OUTCOME

Q: At what age does depression typically begin?

A: With bipolar depression, the first symptoms appear at the average age of just over 15, but treatment is often delayed until the average age of 22.

Q: What is the relationship between mood disorders and premenstrual syndrome (PMS)?

A: One way of looking at PMS is as a recurrent mood disorder that is triggered by the hormonal changes that precede menstruation. About 10 percent of all women have severe PMS. Of those, half have a personal history of depression, and three-quarters have a close relative with major mood disorders. This suggests that PMS and mood disorders are closely related. Many medications used to treat or prevent unipolar or bipolar depressions have a beneficial effect on PMS, as does cognitive therapy. When these measures fail to provide relief, therapy with low doses of danazol is often effective.

Q: Are there any warning signs that suggest that a person might be developing a depression?

A: Prior to the development of a full-blown episode of depression many people show indications that they are on their way to becoming depressed. For some the earliest sign of a developing depression is an increase in anxiety and tension. A change in sleep patterns, irritability, fatigue, difficulty doing everyday tasks or having an indifferent attitude are other possible indicators that a depressive episode is about to begin. People who have had more than one episode of depression usually develop symptoms in the same sequence each time. It is particularly important for relatives to become aware of the symptoms of depression that their family member tends to exhibit. When these symptoms are noticed the family should strongly encourage the patient to contact his psychiatrist for immediate treatment.

Q: It is weird but it seems that I can tell when my wife is getting depressed—sometimes weeks before she herself feels the depression. I can also tell (as can our children) when she begins to respond to treatment, often weeks before she herself recognizes that she is improving. Why is this?

A: There is an old psychiatric aphorism regarding depression that says "Objective changes precede subjective changes." In other words, before people notice changes in their own moods, those around them are often aware of changes in speech patterns, activity levels and interests. It is not unusual for family and friends to notice the onset of a depression and a deterioration of mood often weeks before the depressed individual does. Early treatment of a depressive episode may prevent the depression from becoming severe and prevent much suffering.

Q: Does depression always recur?

A: While some people have just one episode of depression, most of those who have a severe episode of depression will have additional episodes. These additional episodes of depression may be prevented by the long-term use of antidepressants or lithium.

Q: My father acts and looks depressed most of the time and occasionally expresses feelings of hopelessness and says that he would be better off dead. Yet, whenever there are visitors in our home, he manages to look and act like his old undepressed self. Does his ability to seem normal indicate that he really is not all that severely depressed and that we don't have to worry about the possibility of his committing suicide?

A: No! Depressed people can often hide their depression quite effectively. For example, depressed physicians sometimes can hide their depressions from their patients, but make no effort to hide their melancholic moods from their spouses and families. Because people can appear to be entirely "normal" at times by no means implies that they might not be suicidal. They are as likely to kill themselves as anyone else who feels hopeless and threatens suicide.

Q: What are the earliest symptoms that suggest that a person is developing a manic episode?

A: Frequently the earliest indicators of a developing manic episode are decreased need for sleep and an increased activity which often leads to increased productivity at work. Similar to depressions, the symptoms of recurrent manic episodes often develop in the same order with each episode. Since manic episodes are most easily treated at the earliest possible stage, it is important that these initial symptoms be recognized, and that treatment commences rapidly.

Q: In cases of bipolar disorder, do manic and depressive episodes
        usually follow each other in a regular pattern?

A: For most people with bipolar disorder there is no fixed sequence
        in which they experience episodes of depression and mania.
        However, there are some who may show a fixed pattern, for
        example, they experience a manic episode preceding each se-
        vere depression.

Q: My son has had four episodes of depression, including two that
        required him to be hospitalized. Despite his history, he refuses
        to admit that he is ill, and will not accept any treatment. Why is
        this?

A: Many people can accept that they have a mood disorder and
        actively participate in their treatment. Others, however, refuse
        to acknowledge the fact that they are ill in any way. It is impor-
        tant to educate people who deny these problems because their
        denial is often based on the misconception that their illness is an
        indication of weakness and on a fear of others' opinions. This
        may be especially true among young people who simply do not
        know any better and older people who lived in an era when
        "mental problems" were considered repugnant. Even when a
        person's illness has devastating personal effects on them and
        their family, they may continue to deny that they have a prob-
        lem. Not surprisingly, those who are in denial about their prob-
        lems are also reluctant to take medication and also have
        misconceptions about the benefits of medical treatment.

Q: My father has a very severe depression. Although he is a suc-
        cessful businessman with a large and healthy family, he believes
        that he is a pauper and that everyone in the family is dead. His
        psychiatrist says he has a psychotic depression. I am afraid that
        he will spend the rest of his life in a mental hospital. Is it true
        that people with psychotic depression never get better?

A: No, this is not true. Those with psychotic depression generally
        require more intensive treatment than those without delusions,
        but nearly all people with psychotic depression (also called
        delusional depression) respond to one of two treatments, a

combination of an antidepressant and an antipsychotic agent, and bilateral electroconvulsive therapy (ECT).

Q: I have had episodes of mania after returning to the United States from Europe. Is travel a trigger for bipolar disorder?

A: Curiously, it has been shown that east-west travel has a detrimental effect on mood and this is especially true for those with bipolar disorder. The sleep interruption that accompanies such travel may precipitate an episode of mania. One way to minimize the effects of east-west travel on mood is to keep one's clock and schedule synchronized with home time. For those taking lithium (or other medications) it is very important to continue treatment on a regular schedule while traveling.

Q: If I develop serious manic symptoms that cause me to be hospitalized, will I be put in a strait jacket?

A: While the strait-jacket was once used regularly in psychiatric hospitals, it is now rarely used. Patients who once had to be controlled with a strait jacket are now treated intensively with medications so they are no longer a danger to themselves or others. Because drugs have proved to be so effective, restraints are now, for the most part, obsolete.

Q: Why are people who are in manic episodes hospitalized?

A: The most common reasons that cause those in a manic state to be hospitalized are not only that people in a manic state can be a danger to themselves but also because they can be destructive to others. Among the symptoms that cause people to be hospitalized are: spending far too much money, insomnia, overtalkativeness, alcohol abuse, overactivity, hallucinations, delusions, sexual behavior that can be destructive for the person as well as others, and aggression against people or objects.

Q: I have recently become depressed and have started treatment with an antidepressant. Is it possible that I will remain depressed in the future, even with the treatment?

A: The chances are good that you will improve. About 80 percent
         of depressed people who are treated with antidepressants are
         better within 2 years of starting treatment and only approxi-
         mately 1 out of 5 patients fail to improve.

Q: What are some of the effects of depression on one's personality?

A: When depressed, many people complain that they have lost
         their old personalities. Those who are depressed often have little
         interest in anything, get little enjoyment from activities, lack
         enthusiasm and usually are not interested in being with other
         people. When the depression resolves, a person's old personal-
         ity should gradually return.

Q: My wife's depression is beginning to have a bad effect on me
         and I'm afraid that her illness is going to end up destroying our
         marriage. Do other people have this concern?

A: The symptoms of depression often have a catastrophic impact
         and a disruptive effect on an individual's relationships with
         friends and family. When people are depressed they will fre-
         quently not have the interest or energy to keep in contact with
         friends, become inattentive to their family members and lose
         interest in most social activities. When severely depressed, it is
         not unusual for people to socially withdraw to such an extent
         that they stop answering the phone and will not open or answer
         letters. Mania has even more severe effects upon interpersonal
         relationships. Family members, friends and employers who
         understand and are able to tolerate depressed behavior often
         become very intolerant of the loud, impulsive, inappropriate
         behavior that accompanies mania.

Q: I had two episodes of depression while I was in my 20s. I am
         now in my mid-30s and wish to become pregnant. Is it likely that
         I will become depressed during the pregnancy or after the birth
         of my child?

A: Many women, if not most, are not depressed during pregnancy.
         In fact, this period is usually depresssion-free. However, women
         who have a history of depression are more likely to become

depressed following childbirth than women without a history
of depression.

Q: My doctor told me that after 65 some people who have had
mood disorders for a long time are able to become symptom-free
even when their usual medications are discontinued. I am bipolar and would like to know what the chances are that I can give
up my lithium when I reach 65?

A: It is true that after age 65 some people who have had many
episodes of a mood disorder earlier in their lives can remain well
without medications. Approximatley one in three bipolar patients and one in eight unipolar patients may look forward to
this. Unfortunately, for others, the frequency of episodes remains the same and sometimes they increase.

BIOLOGICAL CAUSES

Q: Are mood disorders inherited?

A: Clearly there are some families in which there are more than the
expected number of people with mood disorders. Children born
into such families have an increased likelihood of developing a
mood disorder, even if they are given up for adoption at birth.
That such children develop mood disorders when raised by
adoptive families that are free of mood disorders strongly shows
that the tendency toward developing a mood disorder is inherited.

Q: I have unipolar depression. While there are some depressed
people in my family, my wife and her family are all depression-
free. If my wife and I have children, what are the chances that
our children will inherit my depression?

A: On the basis of inheritance, each one of your children would
have a 17 percent chance of developing a depression at some
point in their lives.

Q: I have had bipolar disorder for 10 years. If I have children are they likely to have the same illness?

A: No. Most children of people who have bipolar disorder will not have a mood disorder, but if they do, chances are that they will develop unipolar disorder rather than bipolar disorder. If your spouse is free of a mood disorder, the risk that your children will develop bipolar disorder is about 7 percent, while the risk of unipolar depression is about 10 percent.

Q: My doctor says that a chemical imbalance causes my depression. What is a chemical imbalance?

A: A chemical imbalance is a simple way of referring to disturbances in brain chemistry that may result in mood disorders.

Q: How does brain chemistry cause mood disorders?

A: In the brain, chemical messengers—known as neurotransmitters—transmit impulses from one nerve cell to another. Serotonin, norepinephrine and dopamine are among the more important neurotransmitters. Neurotransmitters are released by one cell and attach themselves to receptors on the next cell. Disturbances in the amount of neurotransmitters or in the number of receptors appears to be the biological cause of mood disorders.

Q: Specifically, where in the brain are neurotransmitters located?

A: The regulation of neurotransmitter systems that are responsible for mood disorders involves the brainstem, hypothalamus and limbic system. These are the same parts of the brain that control alertness, mood, sleep, sexual behavior and response to stress and memory.

Q: Can nutritional deficiencies cause depression?

A: There is the possibility that severe vitamin deficiencies can cause depression in some people (for example, the elderly, who often have bad eating habits and are especially likely to be deficient in various vitamins and nutrients). It is believed that deficiencies in ascorbic acid (vitamin C), folic acid, niacin (vitamin B_3), pyridoxine (vitamin B_6), riboflavin (vitamin B_2), thiamine (vitamin B_1), and vitamin B_{12} may cause depression. In addition, depression may also possibly result from deficiencies of various minerals including calcium, iron, magnesium, manganese, potassium, sodium and zinc. Vitamin deficiencies by themselves do not play a role in most mood disorders.

Q: When discussing the biological origins of my bipolar disorder, my psychiatrist said something like "biology is fate." Did he mean to imply that I will never be able to master my illness?

A: I think your psychiatrist was trying to point out to you that the basic biological basis of your illness is something that will be with you throughout your life. The extent to which you develop symptoms of bipolar disorder depends to a large extent on you. If you understand your illness, take your medication faithfully, avoid poor sleep habits, alcohol and drug abuse and learn through psychotherapy how to deal with stressful life events, you will be able to minimize the impact of your illness.

Q: I have heavy menstrual periods and my doctor says that I am slightly anemic despite the fact that I take iron tablets. I am almost always tired and depressed. Might my anemia be the cause of my symptoms?

A: Mild anemia seldom causes tiredness and depression. While you should work with your doctor to correct your anemia, it is unlikely that iron therapy will help your depression.

Q: Can any of the drugs used to treat various medical illnesses cause depression?

A: Yes, they can. Drugs from the following categories are known to cause depression:

- Drugs for high blood pressure
- Drugs for heart disease
- Painkillers
- Drugs for stomach and intestinal problems

- Anticonvulsants
- Sedatives and sleeping pills
- Drugs for Parkinson's disease
- Cancer chemotherapy drugs
- Oral contraceptives
- Antibiotics

Q: I have a history of having been depressed on two occasions. What should I do if I need to take medicine that is known to cause depression? For example, I am supposed to take two high blood pressure medications.

A: It is important to alert your physicians to your history of depression. When they are choosing a medication for you, they will choose ones that are not known to cause or increase depression. In some cases, the seriousness of the condition needing treatment and the lack of alternative treatments leaves little choice but to use a drug that may cause depression. If you find yourself in this position, be sure that your psychiatrist is in frequent contact with your other doctors.

Q: Might allergies cause depression?

A: There is no evidence that allergies are responsible for the development of depression.

Q: My father believes that the LSD I took in the 1960s is the cause of my manic-depression. How likely is this?

A: There is no evidence that the use of hallucinogens such as LSD causes bipolar disorder. However, LSD (and other hallucinogens) should not be used by people with mood disorders because they increase the danger of psychotic or suicidal behavior.

PSYCHOLOGICAL CAUSES

Q: If biochemical changes in the brain are so critical in causing depression, why is it that I become depressed mainly when I am under a lot of stress?

A: Certain people become depressed or manic when they are under stress. Stress plays a particularly important role in the onset of the first episode of a mood disorder, but also may be important in precipitating subsequent episodes. There is a good deal of current research on the neurochemical ways in which stress triggers episodes of mood disorders. It is known that stress alters the amount of several hormones in the hypothalamus, and in susceptible individuals these hormonal changes can lead to episodes of depression or mania. An important function of psychotherapy is to help people with mood disorders cope with difficult life situations without becoming depressed or manic.

Q: Are people with certain kinds of personality especially likely to become depressed?

A: Yes. Those with a personality that causes them to be dependent on others, to have difficulty being assertive, to avoid social contact or to have very labile emotions are more prone to depressions than those with other types of personalities.

Q: Does depression cause changes in thinking?

A: Yes, it does. Depressive thinking has the following three major characteristics: negative thoughts about the self; negative thoughts about the world and the people in it; and negative thoughts about the future. These negative thoughts help perpetuate depression. One of the aims of psychotherapy is to help those who are depressed become aware of their tendency to think negatively and to change these thought patterns. Cognitive therapy, a psychotherapeutic technique that focuses on changing such negative thoughts, has been shown to speed recovery from depression.

Q: Some of my friends who are in psychotherapy say that depression comes from anger that is turned inward. Is this really a cause of depression?

A: Not really. Many psychodynamically oriented psychotherapists try to explain depression as anger turned against the self, and while possibly true of some brief depressions, this explanation is not the cause of severe depressions. Research has not shown any evidence that anger turned against the self, or any other psychological mechanism, is the cause of severe mood disorders.

Q: My psychologist says that learned helplessness is a major cause of depression. What is learned helplessness?

A: The learned helplessness theory of depression is based on the idea that when people are depressed they truly believe that there is nothing they can do to change the circumstances that are the cause of the emotional pain they are experiencing. The symptoms of depression are believed to result from this attitude of having no control over life. It is hard to know what is the cause and what is the effect, as the hopelessness that accompanies depression leads people to believe that there is nothing they can do to make themselves feel better.

SOCIAL CAUSES

Q: Is poverty associated with depression?

A: Research has shown that there is some relationship between socioeconomic class and depression and that individuals from socioeconomically deprived backgrounds are more likely to become depressed than those from more privileged backgrounds.

Q: Do loss and grief cause depression?

A: The normal reaction to loss is grief. Grief is usually a self-limited state and usually requires no treatment. At times, the grief process may not resolve itself and is transformed into a depression.

Q: I find that talking to my close friends seems to hold off my depression. What do you think?

A: A study of women and their reactions to difficult life events found that women who lacked an intimate relationship in which they could confide in a friend were four times as likely to become depressed as women who had such a close relationship. In other words, social isolation clearly predisposes people to becoming depressed. If you find that talking and being with people who care about you helps your frame of mind, you should make a point of continuing this type of contact.

SECTION 2

The Treatment of Mood Disorders

GENERAL METHODS

Q: Is it necessary to consult a psychiatrist or are there others who can treat depression?

A: Many different professionals participate in the treatment of depression. Psychiatrists are medical doctors specially trained in the diagnosis and treatment of mental disorders and they conduct their work in hospitals, clinics, community mental health centers and private practice. Psychopharmacologists are psychiatrists who specialize in the use of medications to treat psychiatric disorders. Psychologists and social workers treat depression with psychotherapy and they both work as staff in hospitals and clinics as well as in private practice. Psychiatric nurses work in the inpatient and outpatient departments of general and psychiatric hospitals, community mental health centers and some have private practices. While all of these different types of professionals treat depression and while some physicians can be extremely helpful, only psychiatrists are trained to differentiate depression from other medical disorders and only they can legally prescribe medications. Treatment for depression is available in many settings. For psychiatric emergencies, such as a suicidal crisis, immediate help is available in the emergency rooms of large hospitals. More routine psychiatric care may be obtained in a psychiatrist's private office, in the psychiatric clinic of a general hospital or a community mental health center.

Q: How does one go about finding effective treatment for depression?

A: In my opinion, the first step in getting help is to get an evaluation by a psychiatrist who is experienced in the diagnosis and treatment of depression. Rather than looking in the Yellow Pages, one should seek a psychiatrist who comes well-recommended by a friend or physician whose opinion you trust. When a name is suggested, make sure that the referring person actually knows someone (or preferably several people) whose depression has been treated successfully by that psychiatrist. Avoid referrals where the only comment is something like "I hear this person is a good shrink." If you do not know anyone who can refer you to a psychiatrist, you might try calling the closest medical school or large hospital and asking to speak to someone in the Department of Psychiatry. Tell them that you are looking for a psychiatrist to evaluate your depression and ask if they could recommend at least three.

Q: How are depressions treated?

A: Depressions that are severe enough to cause lack of sleep or appetite or that interfere with functioning at home, work, school or other social situations usually require a combination of psychotherapy and medications. Depressions that are uncomfortable, but do not interfere with sleep, appetite or normal functioning, may respond to psychotherapy alone. If such a depression has not improved after 6 months of psychotherapy, antidepressant therapy should be considered. Too many people remain depressed far longer than they need to because they would rather continue with ineffective psychotherapy than take antidepressant medication.

Q: What can I expect from my first visit to a psychiatrist?

A: On the initial visit most psychiatrists will take a history of your present difficulties, any prior psychiatric symptoms, past medical problems, a family history and a history of drug and alcohol use. Many psychiatrists also find it useful to talk to a close friend or a family member to get additional, objective information about your personality, life situation and illness, if not on the first visit, then soon thereafter. A physical examination and laboratory tests are also conducted to ascertain whether your depression is the result of another illness. This procedure must be done to obtain an accurate diagnosis and before the commencement of any treatment. Obviously not all psychiatrists follow these procedures in the same order, but these basic steps are what you can generally expect on the first visit.

Q: Do insurance companies reimburse patients for the medical treatment of mood disorders or is depression considered to be an emotional problem that does not qualify for reimbursement?

A: How insurance companies regard mood disorders is heavily influenced by the orientation of the treating psychiatrist. For severe mood disorders psychopharmacologists and other biologically oriented psychiatrists often make a diagnosis of cerebral metabolic disorder, a diagnosis based on the belief that severe mood disorders result from alterations in brain function. Insurance companies usually consider cerebral metabolic disorder to be a medical disorder and will reimburse accordingly. When psychiatrists use diagnoses such as major depression or bipolar disorder on insurance forms, insurance companies will usually reimburse at a lower rate than they apply to nervous or mental disorders. Several consumer advocacy groups feel that this policy is not fair and are working toward having psychiatric disorders reimbursed at the same rate as other medical conditions.

Q: My physician has prescribed me antidepressants. What exactly are they?

A: Antidepressants are medications that prevent or relieve depression. These drugs help the brain to produce necessary natural chemicals called neurotransmitters (responsible for the modification or resulting in the transmission of nerve impulses between brain cells) which are often deficient in the brains of depressed people.

Q: Do antidepressants work right away?

A: While some people feel better within 1 week of starting an antidepressant, many find they do not feel the beneficial effects until 2 to 4 weeks after beginning the medication. There are some people who experience a more severely delayed response to the medication and it must be continued, sometimes for 2 months before the severity of the depression is reduced.

Q: I dislike the idea of chemicals altering my brain chemistry and therefore I do not drink alcohol or use drugs. I am depressed now and despite the urging of my psychiatrist, I refuse to take the antidepressants that he recommends. Is there something wrong with my thinking?

A: Serious depression is the result of an alteration in brain chemistry. Antidepressants return brain chemistry to normal; they do not induce an artificial state of mind in the same way that drugs and alcohol do. You should not consider antidepressants as mind-altering substances and you may benefit greatly from taking antidepressants.

Q: My depression has not improved despite psychotherapy and treatment with a number of different antidepressants — four to be exact. Now my doctor wants me to take yet another antidepressant. Does it sound as if he is just trying to take my money, or is there a possibility that another new medication may bring me some relief?

A: It sometimes is necessary to try many antidepressants before finding the one that works for you. An adequate dose that is taken regularly for a long enough period of time is necessary for any antidepressant to work. However, if you find that antidepressants really do not help you, you might consider discussing with your psychiatrist the possibility of electroconvulsive therapy (ECT) which frequently helps those who do not respond to antidepressants.

Q: My doctor has suggested that because I do not respond to antidepressant therapy perhaps I should try electroconvulsive therapy. This treatment sounds scary. What exactly is it and how is it administered?

A: Electroconvulsive therapy (ECT) — usually used for those with acute depression or those who are in immediate and serious danger of suicide — is the induction of a brief convulsion by passing an electric current through the brain. The patient is placed in a comfortable supine position with the limbs lightly restrained. Following premedication and anesthesia, a padded tongue depressor is placed between the teeth to prevent fractures. Electrodes are then placed on both sides of the forehead and a 70 to 130 volt current is delivered for 0.1 to 0.5 seconds. The patient will lose consciousness and will experience muscle contractions. Upon waking, the patient has no memory of the shock. This type of therapy, also called electric shock therapy and electroshock therapy, is usually conducted 3 times a week for 3 or 4 weeks. ECT is usually followed by long-term drug therapy.

Q: I am about to start treatment for depression. How often do psychiatrists usually want to see their patients who they are treating for depression?

A: Psychiatrists usually want to see their depressed patients anywhere from five times a week to once a month. Daily appointments are surely a good idea for those who are severely depressed and suicidal; if they have supportive family members or friends, daily appointments will allow them to remain out of the hospital. When there has been some improvement, the frequency of the visits may be reduced. If there are no suicidal thoughts and the depressed person has an extensive support system, it may be possible to keep this person out of the hospital with many fewer visits. For these more serious types of depression, as treatment progresses, monthly visits may be all that are necessary.

Q: Is there any way that I can monitor my moods so that I can be more aware of the symptoms that indicate the onset of an episode of depression. Would this also be a useful way to follow the progress of my treatment?

A: One simple way to monitor your moods is to fill out symptom checklists for depressed and manic symptoms. The checklists that I use in my practice can be found in the Appendix. These self-administered questions are designed to measure the severity of your depressive and manic symptoms. While high scores indicate the presence of a mood disorder, an actual diagnosis can only be made after a psychiatric interview. You are encouraged to make photocopies for your personal use. The checklists should be completed once a week and the results should be plotted on a chart. The chart below shows the rapid response to an antidepressant.

Week ending	Depression	Mania
2/20/93	39	0
2/27/93	37	0
3/6/93	24	0
3/13/93	11	2
3/20/93	8	4

Scores between 1 and 10 on the checklists for both depression and mania are common when someone is neither depressed nor manic. A score of zero on the depression checklist is often found in people who are hypomanic or manic and a zero score on the mania checklist is often found in people who are severely depressed. Scores of 20 or greater on either scale should be reported to your psychiatrist, as they suggest that your moods may require treatment. High scores on both the depression and the mania checklists are found when someone is in a mixed state. If your doctor does not use checklists like these, you may want to bring your checklists with you to your visits to help your doctor better understand the progress you are making in your treatment. If you complete the checklists each week and include what your current medications are on the sheets, they will become an important record of your treatment and its progress. Also, it is a good idea to continue to keep these records weekly, even when you are feeling well, because they frequently can provide early warning of a change in mood, especially because the checklists can often indicate the onset of a depressive or manic episode well before the change in mood is apparent to you.

Q: I am a photographer and have had episodes of both depression and mania. My psychiatrist wants to start me on lithium, but I do not want to take it because I am afraid that it will decrease my creativity. Is this a real danger?

A: In a study of 24 artists and writers treated with lithium, artistic productivity increased in 12, remained the same in 6 and decreased in 6. Most creative people taking lithium report that they are at least as creative as they were prior to taking lithium. The only artists that reported a decrease in creativity were those who were always in a hypomanic mood prior to the start of lithium therapy.

Q: I have been taking antidepressants for some time. I now want to discontinue these medications and want to know if stopping will cause the recurrence of my depression.

A: Many depressed people can safely stop taking antidepressants after being symptom-free for 6 to 24 months. It is important to remember that antidepressants should never be stopped all at once; the dosage should be gradually reduced and if the depression does not recur, the drug may be tapered off until it is stopped. It is possible, however, that months or years later another course of antidepressant therapy may be necessary because of the onset of another episode of depression. Individuals who have had three or more depressions should discuss with their doctor the possibility of continuous treatment with antidepressants and/or lithium. If tricyclic antidepressants are used in long-term treatment they should be prescribed at full therapeutic doses, not at low maintenance doses.

Q: Can my mood disorder be affected by my diet?

A: There is no evidence that individuals with depression may influence the course of their illness by manipulating their diet.

However, depression due to the deficiency of a nutrient such as vitamin B_{12} may be improved or cured by the administration of the deficient nutrient.

Q: Will a macrobiotic diet help control my mood disorder?

A: There is no evidence that a macrobiotic diet will improve a mood disorder.

Q: My family wants me to see a doctor who specializes in treating psychiatric disorders with, among other medications, mega-doses of vitamins. Will this help speed my recovery from depression?

A: No. There is no evidence that adding megadoses of vitamins to adequate doses of antidepressants speeds recovery from depression.

Q: I've been told that if I am hypnotized and instructed not to have any more depressions, my depressions are likely to disappear. Is this true?

A: No. Although hypnosis is a very useful treatment for some conditions, it is not effective for ending a depressive episode or preventing future episodes of depression.

Q: I am sick and tired of taking antidepressants to control my moods. Can I control my depression with homeopathic remedies or through chiropractic adjustments as has been suggested to me?

A: I can understand your negative feelings about taking medications continuously. Unfortunately, there is no scientific evidence that either homeopathic remedies or chiropractic adjustments have any effect on the course of mood disorders. Just as people with diabetes or an underactive thyroid must take medication for an indefinite period of time, the same is true for some people with depression.

Q: I have been depressed for many years. Some time ago I started taking ginseng and it seems to give me more energy and every time I stop taking it I feel weak and more depressed. Is there any danger in taking ginseng for a long period of time?

A: Although ginseng has been used in the Orient for hundreds of years, its use is not without dangers. One effect of ginseng is the stimulation of the production of adrenal hormones. When one stops taking ginseng, the amounts of these adrenal hormones fall and the reaction that follows as a result may increase depression. Also, there is no scientific evidence that ginseng is a useful treatment for depression.

Q: Why is it that my doctor often prescribes more than one drug at a time to control my depression. Isn't one antidepressant enough?

A: Not always. While most patients require only one antidepressant, when depression resists treatment or is complicated by anxiety, insomnia or a history of mania, there may be a need for more than one medication.

Q: My psychiatrist is treating me with psychotherapy and antidepressants for what he calls a moderately severe depression. He has asked me to make time in my schedule for a brisk walk each day. Is the exercise likely to help me become less depressed, or is he just helping me fill my day?

A: Exercise does have antidepressant effects and depressed patients who exercise regularly may respond more rapidly to antidepressants than those who do not. A 2- to 3-mile walk at least 5 days a week may speed recovery. While it is not clear exactly how exercise helps relieve depression, it may be that it causes the release of endorphins (naturally occurring chemicals that have an antidepressant effect).

Q: I am suffering from bipolar disorder and am now having a severe bout of depression. Is it true that antidepressants may cause me to have a manic episode?

A: The treatment of depressive episodes in bipolar individuals is complicated by the possibility that the antidepressants used to treat the depression may cause the person to have a manic episode. It is as if the drugs do too good a job and elevate the mood beyond a normal level, causing mania. Another complication is that the speed of the cycling between manic and depressed states may be increased. This does not, however, mean that severe depressions in bipolar people should not be treated with antidepressants. Antidepressants such as Wellbutrin, Desyrel (and probably Prozac and Zoloft) are less likely to provoke a manic episode than older antidepressants such as Norpramin or Ludiomil. Depressions in those with bipolar disorder should be treated by psychopharmacologists familiar with the combined use of antidepressants and other mood-regulating medications, such as lithium.

Q: I have been hospitalized over 10 times in the past 14 years for depressions. Is it possible that hospitalizations may become unnecessary for me in the future?

A: The most common reason for repeated hospitalizations for depression is the lack of adequate long-term prophylactic medication. Many patients make the mistake of stopping their antidepressants when they feel well. Patients who have had three or more depressions should make sure that they stay on full therapeutic doses of antidepressants indefinitely to prevent future episodes of depression. (Even if you have not had three or more depressions, you should never take it upon yourself to make the decision to stop your medication; it is imperative that you consult your psychiatrist.) It may be necessary to take antidepressants and lithium, if antidepressants alone do not prevent repeated episodes. For some, depression may require lifelong treatment, similar to the treatment required by those with illnesses such as diabetes and high blood pressure.

Q: If depression results from chemical changes in the brain, why is it that psychotherapy is usually recommended in conjunction with antidepressant therapy?

A: When people are so severely depressed that they require antidepressant treatment, psychotherapy is important to help them deal with the experience of being depressed. Supportive psychotherapy helps relieve the demoralization and hopelessness that accompany depression. Other functions of psychotherapy during acute depressions are to help people accept that they are ill, to give them the strength to excuse themselves from activities they are unable to perform and to help them postpone important life decisions until a better time. Those who become seriously depressed should avoid insight-oriented therapy during the periods in which they are severely depressed; it may increase feelings of hopelessness and demoralization, as well as the possibility of suicide. Most (but unfortunately not all) insight-oriented psychotherapists realize this and switch to supportive psychotherapy when a patient becomes severely depressed.

Q: I suffer from bipolar disorder and my psychiatrist is always stressing that it is important for me to get enough sleep. She has even asked me to let her know if I sleep poorly for just one night. Why is she so concerned about my sleep?

A: Sleep is not only a good indicator of mood, but it also has a major effect on mood. Insufficient sleep can be a major factor in triggering manic episodes. A self-perpetuating cycle begins where the lack of sleep, which leads to mania, leads in turn to even less sleep. Hypomania causes poor sleep and mania then escalates. On the other hand, oversleeping can increase depression.

Q: How does one switch from one antidepressant to another?

A: Changes from one antidepressant to another are usually made gradually. The dose of one drug is reduced and the second drug is then gradually started. When switching from Prozac to a monoamine oxidase (MAO) inhibitor it is necessary for there to be a 5-week period between the time the Prozac is stopped and the MAO inhibitor is started. When switching from most other antidepressants to an MAO inhibitor, a 2-week period between the drugs is all that is needed.

Q: Can people with heart disease safely take antidepressants?

A: For depressed people with heart disease, a psychopharmacologist and cardiologist working together can nearly always agree on the choice of an antidepressant that will be both safe and effective. One danger is that certain antidepressants may cause rhythm disturbances of the heart.

Q: I've been taking an antidepressant for many years. Every time I stop taking it, my depression returns. I am concerned that at some point this drug will stop working. What are the chances of this occurring?

A: Antidepressants nearly always keep working no matter how long one takes them. One change people note when taking antidepressants for many months is that the undesirable side effects gradually diminish. In the rare event that an individual stops responding to one antidepressant, another medication can usually be found that works as well.

Q: I have rapid cycling bipolar disorder and have found that anti-depressants push me into manic episodes. How should my episodes of depression be treated?

A: People with rapidly cycling bipolar disorder should generally be treated without the use of antidepressants. Lithium may be effective in slowing or stopping the cycling process. If it is not, Tegretol or Depakote, either singly or in combination, may help. Sometimes lithium and/or thyroid medication must be added to these medications. At times the use of an antidepressant is unavoidable.

Q: My son stops taking his medications and keeps having severe mood swings that cause him to be hospitalized. Why does he stop taking the medications that are obviously helping him?

A: There are several reasons people stop taking medications that are obviously helpful. Some find the negative side effects intol-erable and would rather risk becoming ill than experience them. It is nearly always possible to find a medication or a combination of medications that will control a mood disorder without caus-ing excessive side effects. Some people stop their medications because they remind them that they are ill. Some people with bipolar disorder like the feeling of their manic highs and do not take medication because they know it will make that feeling disappear. It frequently takes many hospitalizations for such people to realize that their highs are undesirable.

Q: Are different antidepressants used to treat different kinds of depression?

A: All of the available antidepressants are equally effective in treating depressed people. An individual with depression may respond well to one drug and not at all well to others. As a result sometimes several drugs are tried before an effective one is found. "Atypical" depressions accompanied by changeable moods and oversleeping often respond best to MAO inhibitors. Psychotic depressions often respond best to Ascendin, a medication with both antidepressant and antipsychotic actions.

Q: I am depressed and take antidepressants. My doctor wants me to take the same number of pills on the days that I feel bad as I do on days when I feel good. Wouldn't it make sense for me to take more pills on days when I feel depressed and less on better days?

A: No. The number of antidepressant tablets that you take should not fluctuate with the changes in your mood. The effectiveness of antidepressant therapy depends on the amount of medication taken over several weeks. Increasing the dose for a day or two when you do not feel well will not increase the effectiveness of the medication and serves no other purpose whatsoever.

Q: I am depressed and my psychiatrist says that I should start taking antidepressants. I am somewhat overweight and I have heard that I will gain even more weight if I take antidepressant medications. Do they make you gain weight and if so, which antidepressants are least likely to cause weight gain?

A: What you have heard is correct; antidepressants do cause some to gain weight. Prozac, Wellbutrin and Zoloft are the antidepressants least likely to cause weight gain.

Q: When I started taking an antidepressant, my depression got worse as the dose of the medication was increased. Does this mean that I do not respond well to antidepressants and that therefore this type of treatment is not a possibility for me?

A: Occasionally, some people seem to get worse when given certain antidepressants. However, in nearly all such cases a person will respond more favorably to a different drug. Do not make the mistake of thinking that all drugs are the same! Make sure you discuss this carefully with your doctor so that he can come up with an antidepressant that is suitable for you.

Q: When I ask my doctor about my diagnosis or about the side effects of the medications he prescribes for me, his only answer is, "You don't have to know about those things." I really do not agree with his philosophy and feel that I would greatly benefit from more knowledge about my illness and treatment. What should I do to get the information I need to be adequately informed?

A: If your psychiatrist refuses to discuss the details of your illness or your treatment with you, your best bet is to find yourself a new psychiatrist who will provide you with the information you need. If you are being treated in a clinic, request a change of doctor. If necessary, speak directly to the head of the clinic. You have a very valid gripe.

Q: I am taking Tofranil for my depression and Halcion for the insomnia that has been one of the symptoms of my depressions. Since starting these medications I have been repeatedly embarrassed by how poor my memory has become. Can anything be done to improve my memory?

A: Yes there is. While Tofranil can lead to some forgetfulness, Halcion frequently causes brain dysfunction that results in confusion and memory impairment. Let your doctor know about your memory problems and request different medication. She should be able to find a medication that does not disagree with you in the way the Halcion has.

Q: My husband is depressed and refuses to eat the meals I prepare for him. I want him to eat a healthy and balanced diet, but I'm not sure if I should pester him about it. What would you suggest?

A: When people are severely depressed they frequently lose their interest in food. It is not a good idea to argue with depressed people to get them to eat correctly. You should prepare some of your husband's favorite foods and gently encourage him to eat them. If this still does not work and your husband is not eating a balanced diet, you may want to encourage him to take a multivitamin supplement.

Q: When I realize that I am on the verge of a manic episode, what should I do to prevent the development of a really severe bout of manic depression?

A: When you are aware that you are becoming manic, the first thing to do is to call your doctor and arrange an immediate visit. Next, refrain from doing anything that will make the mania worse. It is of utmost importance to reduce stimulation; turn the stereo down and listen to soft, relaxing music instead of hard rock. Any form of stimulation is to a person in a manic episode what gasoline is to a fire. You may find that with the onset of the manic mood you want to engage in many activities and see people, but you should refrain from following through with these impulses. The best advice, even if it sounds harsh, is to place yourself under "house arrest" so to speak, disconnect the telephone and do not leave the house except to see your doctor. Finally, when leaving the house, make sure that you leave most of your cash, credit cards and checks at home to avoid a crazy spending spree which you will only regret later.

Q: My sister has been hospitalized a few times for acute manic episodes. She now lives with my family and is on lithium therapy. We are more than willing to take care of her ourselves and I want to know what we can do to prevent her from requiring hospitalization in the future.

A: If recognized early and treated intensively, a manic episode may often be prevented from progressing to the point where hospitalization is necessary. It is important that you remain alert to the earliest indicators that your sister is beginning to become manic. Irritability and a reduction in the number of hours she usually sleeps are often the first indicators of the onset of a manic episode as are restlessness, increased talkativeness, overactivity, excessive spending and talking on the telephone for extremely long periods of time. If you see any of these symptoms, or any others that you know precede her manic episodes, insist that your sister see her psychiatrist immediately. Do not be surprised if she objects and claims to be fine. You should accompany her on the visit and discuss your observations with her doctor, preferably in her presence. (Her doctor probably will increase her dose of lithium and may add other medications to prevent the mania from becoming worse.) You also can help the situation by protecting your sister from behaviors and situations that seem to worsen her mania, for example, loud music, socializing and long phone calls. You could also protect her from the dangers of overspending money by limiting her access to cash, credit cards and checks.

Q: I have been depressed for almost 2 years and have been treated with many antidepressants that have not helped me very much. Having a few drinks before dinner, wine with dinner and a few after-dinner drinks are among my few remaining pleasures. My psychiatrist tells me that my drinking may be the reason I have not responded to antidepressants. Is he just making excuses for his inability to help me, or is there some reality to what he says?

A: Excessive alcohol intake is a common reason for the lack of response to antidepressant therapy. If we consider a drink to be equivalent to 12 ounces of beer, 4 ounces of wine or 1 ounce of whiskey, you should limit your drinking to two drinks a day. If you are unable to do that, you should not drink at all. Alcoholics Anonymous, Rational Recovery or other self-help groups may help you stop drinking if you are unable to do so on your own.

Q: I think I read somewhere that a form of treatment for depression is staying up all night. Is this kind of enforced wakefulness really used as a treatment for depression and does it work?

A: The practice of limiting sleep time, usually referred to as sleep deprivation, has indeed been used as a treatment method for certain types of depression. Some psychiatric hospitals in Europe keep certain depressed patients awake for one entire night a week because of the belief that sleep deprivation increases the speed with which patients respond to antidepressant therapy. Some psychiatrists have suggested that some of their depressed patients limit themselves to 4 hours sleep during the first half of the night for 2 to 3 nights a week. Sleep deprivation has also been used as a treatment for premenstrual syndrome and rapidly cycling bipolar disorder. Sleep deprivation should only be tried under the supervision of a psychiatrist who is experienced in this kind of treatment as it has been known to induce mania in some.

Q: I have heard many psychiatrists claim that mood disorders should be treated as soon as they are evident. Are there any benefits of postponing treatment for as long as possible or is this dangerous?

A: There is increasing evidence that mood disorders are most responsive to treatment when they first manifest themselves. The longer treatment is delayed, the greater the chance that the disorder will become difficult to control.

Q: Why does it take some people and not others a very long time to recover from an episode of depression? I have been in psychotherapy and have been taking antidepressants for over 2 years and I am still depressed. Is it my fault that I am not better?

A: There are a number of reasons why some people take a long time to respond to treatment: the wrong diagnosis; the incorrect type of psychotherapy; failure of the doctor to prescribe the correct dose of the right antidepressant for an adequate period of time; and the failure to diagnose a medical disorder (such as hypothyroidism) that can interfere with treatment. If you see your psychiatrist regularly, take your medications as prescribed, exercise regularly, do not abuse alcohol or other drugs and make sure you sleep no more than 8 hours a night, you are doing all you can to get over your depression.

Q: What advances in the treatment of depression do you think will be made in the next few years?

A: We are soon likely to see the further development of focused methods of psychotherapy such as cognitive and interpersonal psychotherapy. Additionally, the optimal ways to combine these techniques with psychopharmacologic treatment will become better understood. New drugs, currently under development, will become generally available. Among the drugs that should become available in the United States are some tricyclic drugs that are now available in Europe, an MAO inhibitor, moclobemide, that will require few if any food restrictions, and drugs related to Prozac and Zoloft that may be more effective, yet have fewer side effects.

PSYCHOTHERAPEUTIC TREATMENT

Q: If I take my medications regularly, do I still need psychotherapy for the treatment of my mood disorder?

A: Yes, psychotherapy is an important part of the treatment of mood disorders. Psychotherapy can improve a person's self-esteem and interpersonal relationships (both of which have usually been repeatedly damaged by experiences related to the mood disorder) as well as reducing feelings of isolation. In psychotherapy, dysfunctional attitudes and assumptions about the self and the world are corrected by teaching that these are nonproductive ways of relating to others. Psychotherapy may also help by offering knowledge about mood disorders, explaining the reasons behind the necessity for continuing treatment, overcoming attitudes that interfere with antidepressant therapy and improving methods of coping with difficult life situations, so that episodes of mania or depression will not be triggered.

Q: I have had several depressive episodes and a psychopharmacologist with whom I spoke suggested that I find a therapist who conducts cognitive therapy. What exactly is cognitive therapy?

A: Cognitive therapy is short-term psychotherapy in which the therapist and the patient actively collaborate to identify and eliminate the irrational beliefs and distorted attitudes that perpetuate depression. Many research studies have shown that cognitive therapy is a very effective treatment for depression.

Q: How does cognitive therapy work?

A: Cognitive therapy focuses on teaching the patient to replace distorted, illogical thinking with more rational, realistic thought processes. The end result is that the patient can learn to view herself, the world and the future more accurately. This leads to a more optimistic outlook and better feelings about life in general. Those in cognitive therapy are often asked to tape their sessions so that they can later listen to them. For between-sessions homework, it is also suggested that patients fill out rating forms and record any recurrent negative thoughts that characterize depressive thinking as well as details of any difficult encounters with other people. It is also suggested to patients that they make an effort to engage in pleasurable activities and to read about depression and its treatment. Completing these kinds of homework assignments has been shown to play an important role in speeding the recovery from depression. It is important to be aware that there are many psychotherapists who call themselves "cognitive therapists" or "cognitive-behavioral therapists" who do not have legally proper training. To locate a properly trained cognitive therapist write or phone:

Aaron T. Beck, MD
The Center for Cognitive Therapy
3600 Market Street
Philadelphia, PA 19101
(215) 898-4100

Q: I have been taking antidepressants with moderate success and my psychiatrist wants me to start interpersonal psychotherapy. What is interpersonal therapy and how is it likely to help me?

A: Interpersonal psychotherapy is a focused form of psychotherapy that concentrates on an individual's relationships with others. The emphasis in interpersonal therapy is on solving the interpersonal problems that may cause or increase depression. Interpersonal therapy focuses upon four major areas: losses and personal reactions to losses; disputes with significant others; changes in roles and adaptation to those changes (for example, the transition from being actively employed to being retired); and finally, overcoming social isolation and improving social skills. There is evidence that depressed people who are being treated with both antidepressants and interpersonal therapy, do better than those who only receive one form of treatment or the other. To find a list of therapists who are properly trained in interpersonal psychotherapy contact:

Myrna Weissman, PhD
New York State Psychiatric Institute
722 West 168th Street
New York, NY 10032
(212) 996-6390

Q: My psychiatrist says that he conducts psychoanalytic psychotherapy. How does that differ from cognitive therapy and interpersonal therapy and when and for whom is psychoanalytic psychotherapy useful?

A: Psychoanalytic psychotherapy is a long-term treatment—frequently lasting for many years. In contrast, both cognitive and interpersonal therapies are short-term therapies with which patients can frequently find relief from their depressions in well under a year. Also, whereas psychoanalytic psychotherapy concentrates on the past, interpersonal and cognitive therapies focus on helping the patient find ways to improve the present and the future. Many of those who undergo psychoanalytic psychotherapy complain that the therapy is unfocused and that too much time is wasted discussing things that are unrelated to the depressions that brought them into therapy. Depressed individuals being treated by cognitive or interpersonal therapists usually appreciate that the focus of these types of therapy is on their current difficulties. Psychoanalytic psychotherapy may be useful when a depressed person fails to respond to cognitive and interpersonal psychotherapy.

Q: Although my husband takes his prescribed lithium very regularly, his behavior continues to put a strain on our marriage. I have entered individual psychotherapy in an attempt to understand my reaction to his illness and to improve our relationship. While my therapy has been helpful, we are still having a hard time getting along. What might we do to improve our situation?

A: What you are experiencing is by no means unusual; any chronic illness is more than likely to put a strain on a marriage or other close relationship. Individual psychotherapy for the patient's spouse (which you should be commended for attempting) can often be helpful, but when it is not sufficient, couples therapy, where both partners are seen together, may be more useful.

Q: Is relaxation training useful for people who are depressed or manic?

A: Relaxation training may help some feel more comfortable. While such training may partially reduce depressive or hypomanic symptoms, additional forms of treatment at the same time are necessary. Most people in a full-blown manic state have such poor concentration that they are unable to benefit from relaxation training.

Q: Are there support groups for people with mood disorders?

A: Throughout the United States, Canada and in many other countries there are local groups affiliated with the National Depressive and Manic Depressive Association. If you want to locate a group in your community or you are interested in starting one, contact:

The National Depressive and Manic Depressive Association
Suite 501
730 N. Franklin Street
Chicago, IL 60610
(312) 642-0049
1-800-82N-DMDA

TRICYCLIC ANTIDEPRESSANTS

Q: What are tricyclic antidepressants?

A: Tricyclic antidepressants are used for the treatment and preven-
       tion of episodes of depression. They are also used to treat
       enuresis, panic disorder, bulimia, irritable bowel syndrome,
       chronic fatigue syndrome, migraine headaches and obsessive-
       compulsive disorders.

Q: For the first time in my life I am depressed. My psychiatrist has
       just started me on a medication called Tofranil. How will my
       doctor know what dose of Tofranil will be right for me?

A: For Tofranil to work correctly, there must first be an adequate
       amount in the bloodstream. Interestingly, when two different
       people take the same amount of Tofranil per day, there may be
       great differences in the levels of Tofranil found in each person's
       blood. There are two main ways that the correct dose of Tofranil
       for an individual is determined: (1) a psychiatrist can observe
       the effectiveness of the medication and the magnitude of the side
       effects and (2) he can measure the amount of Tofranil in the
       blood. By determining the amount of Tofranil that is in the
       blood, it is possible to calculate what the lowest necessary dose
       is without taking the risk of causing unnecessary discomfort.

Q: What are some side effects of taking Tofranil and what percent-
       age of people experience these symptoms?

A: Dry mouth is experienced by 30 percent of the people taking
       Tofranil; 25 percent experience dizziness and drowsiness; 20
       percent experience constipation, weight gain, sweating, tremors
       and insomnia; and 15 percent experience blurred vision and
       fatigue.

Q: I have been taking Tofranil and Elavil and am very constipated.
       What can I do to relieve the constipation?

A: Constipation is a common side effect of tricyclic antidepressants, but laxatives should be avoided. Some of the measures that you may find useful in controlling tricyclic-induced constipation are: drinking at least six 8-ounce glasses of water every day; taking Metamucil twice a day; adding 4 or 5 heaping tablespoons of unprocessed bran to your diet (it is most palatable when added to hot or cold cereal); walking briskly for at least 30 minutes each day; and taking a stool softener such as Colace two or three times a day. While some people will need to take all five of these measures, most people only need to take two or three of these suggestions to alleviate the symptoms.

Q: I have been taking up to 200 mg of Tofranil each day for nearly 2 months now. My depression is a little better, but I still feel very depressed. I had a blood test to measure the amount of Tofranil in my blood. My doctor says that the result indicated that the amount of antidepressant in my blood was in the therapeutic range. Since I have few side effects from the Tofranil, he thinks that it is worthwhile to see if I respond better to a higher dose. Do you think 300 mg per day is too much or do you think it might actually help?

A: There are some people who only respond to antidepressants when they have greater than the usual amounts in their blood. If you are tolerating 200 mg of Tofranil without excessive side effects, you very well might become less depressed if your dose is increased to 300 mg a day. Some people require doses of Tofranil as high as 500 mg per day.

Q: I have been taking Tofranil for 6 months now and as a result I feel much less depressed. My doctor tells me that since I have had four previous depressions, I should remain on a full dose of Tofranil indefinitely. Do you agree?

A: People with a history of many depressions may remain depression-free by continuing to take a full dose of Tofranil for long periods of time. If depressions recur despite the Tofranil, adding lithium often is effective.

Q: When I complain of the bad side effects that I get from the
        medication I am taking, my doctor will switch me from one
        antidepressant to another even after I have only been taking that
        medication for a few days. How long should one remain on an
        antidepressant before giving up on it and trying another one?

A: Some physicians are reluctant to keep patients on antidepres-
        sants that cause negative side effects, and effective doses of
        tricyclic antidepressants nearly always have some mild side
        effects such as dry mouth, increased sweating and constipation.
        However, if a tricyclic is stopped each time side effects develop,
        successful treatment with tricyclic antidepressants would never
        be possible. One unfortunate aspect of antidepressant therapy
        is that unpleasant side effects usually manifest before the ther-
        apeutic effects do. If you take tricyclic antidepressants, you
        should be prepared to tolerate some dry mouth, sweating and
        constipation. It should help you to hang in there by remember-
        ing that after taking an antidepressant for a month or so, the side
        effects often become less severe.

Q: Why is thyroid medication sometimes prescribed with tricyclic
        antidepressants?

A: Some people who do not respond to usual doses of tricyclics will
        often respond better if they take thyroid hormones in conjunc-
        tion with the tricyclic.

Q: Do tricyclic antidepressants have an effect on memory?

A: When used in high doses, tricyclic antidepressants may indeed
        cause some problems with memory. Those over the age of 65
        who are taking antidepressants are especially prone to memory
        loss.

Q: I have a history of depression and I also now have developed
        glaucoma. I have been treated in the past with Elavil. Can I still
        take the Elavil now that I have glaucoma?

A: Elavil should not be taken by people with certain types of
        glaucoma. Before you take an antidepressant, it is important for

your ophthalmologist and your psychiatrist to discuss your situation.

Q: I have been taking Elavil for about 5 years. At first it worked well, but recently I have been developing frequent depressions. What will make me feel better now that Elavil does not seem to help me anymore?

A: If Elavil no longer gives you protection from depressions, you probably should be switched to another medication and there are many possibilities. You might do better with another tricyclic antidepressant, a newer antidepressant such as Prozac or Zoloft or possibly lithium.

Q: I am taking Norpramin and it gives me a very dry mouth. Is there anything that I can do to feel more comfortable?

A: Taking frequent sips of water or chewing gum should give you some relief. If the dry mouth is really a major problem for you, you might ask your doctor to prescribe bethanechol, a drug that stimulates the salivary glands to produce saliva. Also, Humibid, a medication usually used to increase bronchial secretions, will often relieve dry mouth. Ask your doctor about these medications.

Q: When taking both Tofranil and Elavil, I have experienced problems with low blood pressure, making me dizzy and faint. Are there any antidepressants that are not likely to lower my blood pressure?

A: It is true that when taking tricyclic antidepressants such as Tofranil and Elavil, some people will experience marked decreases in blood pressure. The newer antidepressants (especially Prozac, Wellbutrin and Zoloft) can often be tolerated by people who developed low blood pressure from tricyclic antidepressants.

Q: Ever since I have been taking Elavil, I have been gaining weight, although I have not changed my diet or the amount of exercise I am getting. Why is this?

A: There is evidence that some people taking tricyclic antidepressants burn fewer calories than they normally would. This change in metabolism can usually be compensated for by reducing food intake and increasing exercise.

Q: Now and then I forget to take a dose of Elavil. What should I do when I miss a dose?

A: If you forget a dose of Elavil you should take it as soon as you remember. If you are taking all your Elavil once a day at bedtime, do *not* take a bedtime dose the next morning as it may cause drowsiness and other uncomfortable effects when taken early in the day.

Q: I have been depressed four times in the past. Each time I was treated with Norpramin and it took about 3 months for me to feel better. When I recently became depressed, my psychiatrist started me on both Norpramin and Prozac and I felt better within 2½ weeks. Is the use of this combination new?

A: Generally, psychiatrists like to treat patients with as few medications as possible. While single drugs often work well, there are some patients who do best on a combination of antidepressants or when drugs such as lithium or thyroid hormones are prescribed along with an antidepressant. Recently, some psychiatrists have been prescribing Prozac combined with a tricyclic antidepressant such as Norpramin. These combinations often relieve depression more rapidly than a single drug.

Q: I have been taking several antidepressants for a severe depression. Recently I was feeling especially suicidal and my doctor and I decided that I should get electroconvulsive therapy. In preparation for the ECT, my antidepressants were stopped. Within a week after stopping the antidepressants, my depression and the suicidal thinking disappeared and I felt well. What happened?

A: When antidepressants are discontinued in someone who has an active depression, it usually causes the depression to worsen, or at best, to stay the same. Occasionally a rapid improvement or even a switch into mania or hypomania is seen. The neurochemical basis for this unexpected change in mood is not well understood.

MONOAMINE OXIDASE INHIBITORS

Q: My doctor wants me to start taking Parnate, a drug he refers to as a monoamine oxidase (MAO) inhibitor. What is monoamine oxidase and why should I take a drug that inhibits it?

A: Monoamine oxidase (MAO) is an enzyme that is found in many parts of the body, including the brain. In the brain, MAO destroys neurotransmitters such as norepinephrine and serotonin. It has been known for many years that drugs that inhibit the action of monoamine oxidase act as antidepressants when given in adequate amounts for a sufficiently long period of time.

Q: When are MAO inhibitors prescribed?

A: MAO inhibitors are the preferred treatment for people with atypical depressions. These medications are also useful for treating people whose depressions have not responded to other antidepressants, depressed older people, especially those with Alzheimer's disease, as well as those who experience frequent panic attacks. MAO's anti-anxiety effects are also especially helpful for anxiety associated with phobia. They are also used in the treatment of migraine headaches and hypertension. Unfortunately, many depressed people are labeled as having a treatment-resistant depression when treatment with an MAO inhibitor has never been attempted.

Q: I have just begun treatment with an MAO inhibitor. My doctor has increased the dose every few days. Is this a normal procedure or am I just a difficult case?

A: Psychiatrists usually prescribe 1 or 2 tablets of an MAO inhibitor on the first day and then increase the dose by 1 tablet every 2 or 3 days until the patient has reached a dose of 3 or 4 tablets daily. Occasionally 10 or more tablets a day will be needed to bring about complete relief from depression.

Q: I am taking the MAO inhibitor Nardil, and my doctor wants me
         to have a blood test to determine if I am taking the correct dose.
         How will the test indicate whether I am on the right dose and
         why is it necessary?

A: Used to measure the amount of monoamine oxidase that is
         active in the blood, this test is used to determine if an adequate
         dose of MAO inhibitor is being taken. This is important because
         many depressed people fail to respond to MAO inhibitors sim-
         ply because they are not taking a sufficient dose. The MAO
         blood test is available only in some cities. When it is not avail-
         able, the best ways to determine if the correct dose of Nardil is
         being taken are: (1) body weight (1 mg of Nardil for every 2.2
         pounds) and (2) the response of the depression to treatment.

Q: When depressed I become lethargic and sleep for as much as 14
         hours a day. I have been treated with a few tricyclic antidepres-
         sants without improvement. A physician told me that people
         who oversleep the way I do often respond well to the combina-
         tion of an MAO inhibitor and lithium. Should I accept her
         suggestion or would I be better off with a single antidepressant
         such as Prozac or Zoloft?

A: If your depressions cause lethargy and oversleeping, you will
         probably respond best to treatment with MAO inhibitors. While
         it is possible that you might respond to Prozac or Zoloft, there
         is a better chance that you will respond to the combination of an
         MAO inhibitor and lithium.

Q: My doctor told me that because I am taking an MAO, I should
         not eat certain foods, including, for example, aged cheeses. One
         day, before I realized what I was doing, I ate a Swiss cheese
         sandwich. Much to my surprise, I had no reaction of any kind.
         Does this mean that I can safely eat Swiss cheese in the future?

A: The severity of the reaction to eating certain foods depends on
         the amount of tyramine in the foods. One portion of Swiss
         cheese, for example, may be nearly tyramine-free, while the
         same portion of another brand of Swiss cheese can contain
         sufficient tyramine to cause a severe reaction. You should avoid

all Swiss cheese as you have no way of predicting how much
tyramine will be in it.

Q: I have read that there are some cheeses that safely may be eaten
by people taking MAO inhibitors. Which cheeses are safe?

A: Soft, non-aged varieties such as Boursin, cream cheese, cottage
cheese, Ricotta and Cheez Whiz are generally safe.

Q: Which foods are the most important for me to avoid while
taking a monoamine oxidase inhibitor?

A: The most important foods to avoid are: pickled herring, aged
cheeses, sausages (frankfurters are OK), processed meats such
as corned beef and pastrami, fava beans, sauerkraut, Marmite,
Bovril, large amounts of chocolate (especially European choco-
lates) and any food that may be overripe or that may be on the
verge of going bad. Be sure to ask your doctor for a printed list
of foods that you should avoid.

Q: Is it ever safe for a person who takes MAO inhibitors to drink
alcoholic beverages?

A: Some alcoholic beverages, especially red wines (and particularly Chianti) should be totally avoided by those taking MAO
inhibitors because of the possibility that they will severely raise
blood pressure. Vermouth also should be completely avoided.
Up to 4 ounces of white wine may be consumed per day.
Whiskey, rum, vodka and gin contain hardly any tyramine, but
should be limited to 2 ounces a day because the effects of alcohol
are intensified by an MAO inhibitor.

Q: I understand that besides foods there are both prescription and
over-the-counter drugs that people taking MAO inhibitors
should avoid. Which over-the-counter drugs should I avoid?

A: Avoid nasal decongestants, nose drops, sinus medications, cold
tablets and most asthma inhalers. You should not take any
cough medication that contains dextromethorphan (plain
Robitussin is safe). Consult your physician before you take any

prescription or over-the-counter drugs. It is of utmost importance for you to tell any doctor who is about to prescribe medication for you that you are on an MAO inhibitor. If you find
yourself in a position that requires surgery, make sure to tell the
surgeon and the anesthesiologist that you are taking an MAO
inhibitor and that you cannot take Demerol. When going to the
dentist make sure it is understood that if you require Novocaine
it does not contain epinephrine. Prozac, Wellbutrin and Zoloft
should not be taken for at least 2 weeks after taking an MAO
inhibitor.

Q: My psychiatrist wants me to take Parnate, but I have been
carrying his prescription around with me for a week and am
afraid to fill it because I fear I may accidentally eat the wrong
thing. In your experience, just how dangerous is it to take an
MAO inhibitor.

A: I personally have prescribed MAO inhibitors for over 600 patients. Five of them have had reactions severe enough to require
treatment in a hospital emergency room. Aged cheeses caused
two of the reactions, one was caused by eating a pastrami
sandwich, one by shrimp salad that had not been properly
refrigerated, and one by eating very large amounts of chocolate.
None of these patients suffered any permanent harm from these
reactions. My suggestion to you is to be careful about what you
cannot eat and fill the prescription; it may really help! In other
words, the benefits of taking MAO inhibitors far outweigh the
risks.

Q: My psychiatrist says that I have an atypical depression and has
prescribed Nardil. What side effects might I experience?

A: Nardil is an MAO inhibitor that behaves like any other drug in
this class. The specific side effects of Nardil and the percentage
of users reporting these symptoms are as follows: 20 percent
experience reduced blood pressure, insomnia, decreased sexual
functioning and weight gain; 15 percent experience blurred
vision, dry mouth, rapid pulse and lightheadedness.

Q: I worry about the possibility of gaining weight while taking an MAO inhibitor. Which MAO inhibitor is least likely to lead to weight gain?

A: Parnate is associated with much less weight gain than other antidepressants. About one-third as many people gain weight when taking Parnate as those taking Nardil or Marplan.

Q: I am taking Parnate and my doctor has given me some capsules of Procardia to take if I have a reaction from accidentally eating the wrong foods. Other than developing a headache — a symptom he told me I could probably anticipate — what other symptoms might I develop if I have a reaction?

A: A pounding headache, sweating, chest pain, chills and palpitations, together with a rise in blood pressure are some of the symptoms that develop when someone on an MAO inhibitor eats food rich in tyramine. Taking Procardia is first-aid for such a reaction. It is possible that the Procardia will control your blood pressure for an hour or so, but the pressure may become dangerously high when the effects wear off. Because of this, it is important that you go to a hospital emergency room if you ever have a hypertensive reaction.

Q: Is it true that MAO inhibitors may cause a depressed bipolar person to become manic?

A: Like tricyclic antidepressants, there is some risk of mania when a person with bipolar disorder takes an MAO inhibitor; however, taking lithium or another mood-stabilizing drug with the MAO inhibitor minimizes this risk.

Q: Since starting Parnate about 2 months ago I became very tired in the late afternoon. I try to avoid caffeine and wonder what might be done to control this unpleasant side effect?

A: What you are experiencing is not unusual; MAO inhibitors are frequently associated with late afternoon tiredness. Many people taking MAO inhibitors have found that a 20-minute nap in the middle of the afternoon can be wonderfully refreshing. Try not to sleep for more than half an hour so as not to interfere with your night-time sleep.

Q: Are MAO inhibitors ever used in combination with tricyclic antidepressants?

A: Psychiatrists sometimes prescribe a tricyclic antidepressant in combination with an MAO inhibitor. The chief use of this combination is in people whose depressions have resisted less complex treatments.

NEWER ANTIDEPRESSANTS

Q: My psychiatrist wants me to take Prozac because of depression, but I am afraid to start because of what I have read about its side effects. Just what are the side effects of Prozac and how common are they?

A: Most people find that Prozac is an easy medication to take. When they do occur the side effects are usually mild and transient. Some of the more common side effects of Prozac and the percentage of users who have reported having them are: 30 percent report dry mouth; 25 percent report restlessness and nervousness; 20 percent report nausea or vomiting, weight loss, headache, decreased sexual functioning and insomnia; 15 percent report fatigue/sedation, weight gain and diarrhea; and 15 percent report experiencing tremors.

Q: Which antidepressant is least likely to cause a manic episode for a depressed bipolar person?

A: Bupropion, sold under the trade name Wellbutrin, is the antidepressant least likely to induce a manic episode.

Q: Soon after starting Prozac, the first antidepressant that helped me, I stopped having orgasms. Can I do anything to improve this situation, other than stopping the Prozac?

A: Reducing the dose of Prozac may help. If it does not, your doctor can prescribe either Periactin or bethanechol which you should take 45 to 60 minutes before having sex. These medications frequently restore the ability to climax during sex.

Q: Since starting Prozac I have had a very hard time falling asleep. What can be done for my insomnia?

A: Usually the antidepressant Desyrel (25 to 100 mg) does an excellent job of counteracting the insomnia some people develop when taking Prozac or Zoloft. The Desyrel should be taken about 30 to 45 minutes before you try to sleep.

Q: I have read awful accounts about people who were taking Prozac becoming suicidal. Is this true?

A: Almost 5 million people have taken Prozac in the United States and there have been some suicides among them, as would be expected of any depressed population. Prozac makes some people very agitated and if they are already suicidal, this agitation is sometimes all it takes to cause suicidal behavior. There is no evidence that people kill themselves more often while taking Prozac than while taking any other antidepressants.

Q: My depression has responded well to Prozac. While my doctor wants me to continue taking it for a few more months, I took it upon myself to stop taking it 2 weeks ago and I'm still feeling fine. Was I correct in stopping the Prozac?

A: Because you are not depressed 2 weeks after stopping Prozac does not mean that you no longer require the medication. Prozac is a drug that remains in the blood for a month or so after you stop taking it. It is possible that you continue to feel well because of the action of the Prozac that still remains in your body. Prozac, like other antidepressants, should be continued for at least 6 months after a depression remits.

Q: I have tried taking various tricyclic drugs and my depression has not responded well to any of them. I am now taking Prozac and it seems to be helping a little. My doctor thinks that adding lithium to the Prozac will make the Prozac work better. Is he right that this combination will likely help me get over my depression?

A: There are many ways to augment the antidepressant actions of the primary drugs used to treat mood disorders. Among the drugs used to augment Prozac are tricyclic antidepressants (such as Norpramin and Pamelor) and lithium.

Q: I have had four severe bouts of depression. My most recent episode was treated with Prozac and I responded well. My doctor now wants me to remain on Prozac in order to prevent future depressions. Has long-term Prozac treatment been shown to prevent depressions?

A: Just as long-term administration of therapeutic doses of Tofranil has been shown to prevent depressive relapses, the same has been shown to be true for Prozac. In one study, depressed individuals maintained on Prozac (40 mg a day) had few depressive relapses.

Q: Prozac did a good job of controlling my depression but I gained 40 pounds and had sexual difficulties while taking it. Is there any antidepressant that will not cause weight gain and loss of sexual drive?

A: Of the available antidepressants, Wellbutrin is least likely to cause weight gain and sexual problems.

Q: Since taking Prozac my depression has improved greatly, but I am sleepy a lot of the time. Is there any way I might continue to benefit from this drug without the sleepiness?

A: Some people can counteract the sleepiness by increasing their intake of caffeine. Taking short naps can also help considerably.

Q: I am on lithium and Prozac and have developed sexual potency problems and my doctor wants to give me yohimbine to reverse them. Is yohimbine effective in this situation?

A: Yohimbine is often successful in reversing the sexual problems caused by antidepressants including Prozac. One problem with yohimbine is that it can induce mania in some bipolar people. Therefore, if you are on lithium because of mania or hypomania, you should avoid yohimbine. Urecholine, Periactin and Symmetrel have also been effective in reversing antidepressant-induced sexual problems.

Q: Is Prozac safe for elderly people with heart trouble?

A: While there is only preliminary evidence so far, it appears that Prozac has far fewer side effects related to the heart than most other antidepressants. Although there are a few reports of elderly people with cardiac disease developing heart symptoms on Prozac, such reports are rare.

Q: I am now taking lithium and my psychiatrist wants me to take Zoloft with the lithium because I am still depressed. Is there a danger that the Zoloft will have any effect on my lithium level?

A: While many drugs including Prozac may change lithium levels, Zoloft is free of any such effect. In other words, the combination is safe.

Q: My depressions did not respond to many different antidepressants until I started taking Wellbutrin. It has improved my depression but it makes me anxious. What can I do about this anxiety?

A: Sometimes a slight reduction in the dose of an antidepressant is all that is necessary to eliminate a side effect. If that does not work, you might ask your doctor to treat your anxiety with small doses of an anti-anxiety agent such as Ativan or Xanax.

Q: My doctor wants to start me on Wellbutrin to treat my depression. Will this drug have the same side effects as the others I have taken?

A: Wellbutrin is usually an easy drug to take as it has few side effects. The most common side effects are: 30 percent report restlessness/nervousness; 20 percent report decreased appetite, weight loss and dry mouth; 15 percent report nausea and vomiting, sweating, constipation, blurred vision and headache; and 10 percent report tremors.

Q: I have been depressed and sleeping badly for about 5 months. My psychiatrist recently started me on Desyrel and told me that if I take it at bedtime, it is likely to help both my sleep and mood. He also mentioned that when I have an erection while on this drug I might find that it will take much longer than usual to subside. What is the connection between Desyrel and erections?

A: A few men taking Desyrel have developed inappropriate erections or have had erections that resolve much more slowly than usual. However, fewer than 1 in 20,000 men taking Desyrel will develop an erection that will not resolve on its own. However, this situation is a medical emergency and should be treated immediately at a hospital emergency room.

Q: I have been taking Prozac for several months. At a recent meeting of my Mood Disorders Support Group some people said that they had been taken off Prozac and started on Zoloft. Is one drug better than the other?

A: Both Prozac and Zoloft have powerful effects on the chemical systems of the brain. They are both highly effective antidepressants with far fewer side effects than the older antidepressants. Another advantage is that it is less likely to cause agitation than Prozac. On the other hand, Prozac is less likely to cause nausea and diarrhea than Zoloft. In women, Zoloft causes less sexual dysfunction than Prozac. However, Prozac has been available for many more years than Zoloft and psychiatrists have had more experience with it.

Q: I have been depressed for a long time and have not responded to a number of antidepressants. When I recently visited my doctor he wanted me to start taking Paxil. What is Paxil and what side effects might I expect from it?

A: Paxil is a recently developed antidepressant. Its mode of action is similar to that of Prozac and Zoloft. The most common side effects are nausea, sleepiness, dry mouth and constipation. Less frequent side effects include dizziness, ejaculatory problems, insomnia, diarrhea and sweating.

LITHIUM

Q: What is lithium and when is it prescribed?

A: Lithium is a naturally occurring substance that is mined from the earth. It is usually prescribed as tablets or capsules of lithium carbonate—a compound easily absorbed by the body. The chief indications for lithium are for the treatment of acute manic episodes, the long-term prophylaxis of unipolar depression and bipolar disorder, the potentiation of antidepressants and the prevention of cluster headaches. Other uses of lithium include the treatment of schizoaffective disorder, borderline personality disorder, premenstrual mood syndrome, alcoholism and aggression.

Q: I have had four spells of depression, but I have never been manic. I recently recovered from an episode of severe depression. My doctor wants me to take lithium for an indefinite period to prevent future depressions. Is this advisable?

A: Lithium is an effective treatment for many mood disorders, not just bipolar disorder. It frequently helps people with unipolar depressions. During the treatment of acute episodes, lithium helps antidepressants work more effectively. It will also help prevent the recurrence of unipolar episodes.

Q: What is involved in starting lithium therapy?

A: After it is decided that someone should start taking lithium, it is important to determine if there is any medical condition that would make lithium therapy dangerous. Blood and urine tests are done routinely, as is an electrocardiogram for persons over the age of 50.

Q: When taking lithium, how often must I go for a lithium blood test?

A: The frequency with which one should have lithium blood level determinations differs from person to person and from time to time in a given patient. At the start of lithium therapy patients may be asked to get lithium levels measured as often as every 5 to 10 days. As therapy progresses, especially when the lithium blood level is consistent, the tests are done at longer intervals. Ultimately, patients who have taken lithium for many years may require only one or two lithium tests a year.

Q: Over the years my doctors have given me confusing instructions about how to get a lithium test. What is the proper timing between taking the lithium dose and having blood drawn for a lithium level? Also, can I eat prior to having a lithium test?

A: Blood for lithium tests should be drawn exactly 12 hours after the last dose of lithium. "Exactly" in this situation means that your blood should be drawn between 11½ and 12½ hours after your last dose. For example, if you took lithium at 11 at night, blood must be drawn precisely between the hours of 10:30 and 11:30 the next morning. If you are having only a lithium test, you may eat prior to having blood drawn.

Q: Are there problems with staying on lithium therapy?

A: Lithium treatment must be monitored by regular visits to the doctor who prescribed it. Besides observing the effects of the lithium, your doctor will want you to periodically have tests taken to determine the amount of lithium that is in your blood. The optimal amounts of lithium in the blood are known and these blood tests ensure that the dose of lithium you are taking is right for you. Every 6 to 12 months, kidney, thyroid and parathyroid functions are tested as they may be affected by lithium.

Q: Are there certain people with bipolar disorder who are more likely to be helped by lithium?

A: People whose manic states are clearly euphoric are more likely to respond to lithium than those whose manias are characterized by irritability. Rapid cyclers—individuals with four or more mood episodes per year—are less likely to do well than bipolar patients who have fewer episodes per year. People whose sequence of mood states is manic-depressed-normal generally respond better to lithium than people whose sequence is depressed-manic-normal.

Q: What percentage of people with bipolar depressions benefit from taking lithium?

A: About 80 percent of those with bipolar illness respond either totally or partially to lithium treatment. About one third of people with bipolar disorder never have an episode of mania or depression while taking lithium and approximately 50 percent have fewer, milder or less frequent episodes. Most of the 20 percent who receive no benefit from lithium therapy will respond to other medications such as Tegretol or Depakote.

Q: Besides lithium my doctor has prescribed Stelazine, Prolixin and Haldol at various times. I have heard that people with bipolar disorder should avoid these drugs. Is this true?

A: All of the drugs you mention are antipsychotic medications—drugs that have the capacity to permanently damage the central nervous system. The damage may lead to tardive dyskinesia, which shows up as involuntary movements of the face or other parts of the body. Although antipsychotics are sometimes useful in the treatment of bipolar disorder, their use should be minimized. While anyone taking antipsychotics may develop tardive dyskinesia, persons with mood disorders are more susceptible to it than those with schizophrenia.

Q: I have been diagnosed as having cyclothymia and have been taking lithium for 6 months, but there has been no change in the frequency or severity of my mood swings. How long will it take for lithium to control my mood swings?

A: Cyclothymia, a mild form of mood disorder, may be slow to respond to lithium therapy. You should take lithium for 12 to 18 months before your doctor can decide whether it will be useful or not.

Q: I have been having mood swings for about 20 years and have always refused treatment. Because I have postponed treatment for so long, have I reduced the possibility that lithium will help me?

A: The more episodes of bipolar disorder a person experiences, the more difficult it becomes to control. However, even patients who have had dozens of episodes have a good chance of responding to lithium or other medications that control mood swings. It is worthwhile to start treatment regardless of how many times or for how long you have had mood swings.

Q: For many years lithium has controlled my rapid cycling bipolar disorder. It has recently stopped working to some extent and I am now having more frequent episodes. What can be done about this?

A: The addition of Tegretol or Depakote to the lithium is likely to bring this problem under control.

Q: My doctor tells me that my lithium level is 0.8. She wants to increase it to a bit over 1.0 with a higher dosage because I am continuing to have mood swings. Is this strategy a useful one?

A: Although many patients do best with a lithium blood level of about 0.8, there are others who require higher lithium levels to prevent manic and depressive episodes. However, levels above 2.0 are associated with adverse reactions.

Q: Does lithium work as an antidepressant?

A: Lithium was introduced to terminate manic and hypomanic episodes. However, it frequently has antidepressant effects, which may be seen in both unipolar and bipolar patients.

Q: I have been diagnosed as having manic-depression and despite the fact that I take lithium, I still have mood swings. I am disappointed as I expected the lithium to control my mood swings completely. Why didn't the lithium therapy work for me?

A: In people with bipolar disorder, there is a spectrum of responses to lithium therapy. Lithium totally controls the mood swings of some people, partially controls the mood swings in others and lacks effect completely in a small number. If your mood swings are being only partially controlled, you may want to ask your doctor if adding Tegretol or Depakote to lithium might benefit you.

Q: When starting me on lithium, my doctor told me not to eat Chinese food more than once a week. What is this all about?

A: In addition to excreting lithium, the kidney also excretes salt into the urine. When one eats foods that are rich in salt, such as Chinese food, the kidney rids the body of sodium by increasing the amount of salt excreted in the urine. The kidney has a hard time telling sodium from lithium and when a large amount of sodium is excreted, a large amount of lithium is also excreted. By avoiding excessive amounts of salt in your diet you prevent the kidneys from excreting large amounts of lithium and avoid a fall in the lithium level. On the other hand, eating a low-salt diet while taking lithium may also be dangerous. When there is insufficient sodium in your diet, the kidneys excrete little very lithium, allowing it to accumulate in the blood, which in turn can lead to lithium toxicity.

Q: What are the early warning signs that I may have too much lithium in my blood?

A: When the level of lithium in the blood becomes too high, the first indicators are usually difficulty concentrating, nausea, diarrhea and tremors. If the lithium level continues to increase, slurred speech, vomiting, blurred vision, dizziness, muscle twitches, drowsiness, being unsteady on one's feet, disorientation and confusion may be experienced. If these symptoms develop, stop the lithium and immediately contact your doctor. The best ways to prevent lithium toxicity are to have regular lithium blood level determinations, ensure adequate liquid intake, especially in hot weather, and avoid salt depletion when working or playing strenuously.

Q: I am on lithium and in the summer I perspire a lot when working or playing hard. Is my heavy perspiration likely to have any effect on my lithium level?

A: Heavy sweating results in salt loss and this can lead to an increase in the blood level of lithium. When working or playing hard in hot weather it is very important to have an adequate intake of water and salt. Drinks such as Gatorade may be useful in helping you replace lost water and salt.

Q: How often does one take lithium?

A: Lithium, especially when taken as a sustained-release tablet (Lithobid), is usually taken once or twice a day. When lithium is taken once a day it has fewer adverse effects upon kidney function.

Q: What side effects may I experience once I begin to take lithium?

A: During the first week or so of lithium therapy you may notice some nausea and diarrhea. You also might become aware of some tremors of your hands and a sensation of fatigue. These side effects usually disappear in a week to 10 days. If they persist longer than that, or recur at some later point in your treatment, be sure to notify your doctor.

Q: What can I do if about the nausea I experience immediately after I take each dose of lithium?

A: Nausea immediately following a dose of lithium is caused by the effects of lithium on the stomach. Try taking lithium immediately after eating a meal or switching to long-acting lithium tablets; this will usually eliminate the nausea. With long-acting tablets, most of the lithium is released after the pill passes through the stomach.

Q: Are all lithium preparations alike? I have a lot of trouble with the pills.

A: Lithium is available in long-acting tablets, capsules and a liquid preparation. Some people find that they can tolerate one of these preparations better than the others. Each of these lithium preparations is equal in its ability to control mood disorders.

Q: Is it true that the lithium level in my blood can rise as a result of other medications such as Motrin, which I take for arthitis.

A: Yes. Some drugs do increase lithium levels and must be taken with caution. These include:

- Diuretics
- Ampicillin
- Capoten
- Phenylbutazone
- Naproxen
- Metronidazole
- Tegretol
- Erythromycin
- Spectinomycin
- Enalapril
- Mefanamic acid (Ponstel)
- Indocin
- Ibuprofen (Advil, Motrin)
- Dilantin
- Mazindol
- Tetracycline
- Methyldopa

Q: While I am taking lithium must I give up alcohol?

A: Although small amounts of alcohol can be taken with lithium, its use should be minimized by people with mood disorders. Excessive use of alcohol can lead to mood swings and prevent an individual from responding to treatment. Also, patients with mood disorders are very much at risk for developing alcoholism and other forms of drug abuse. Abuse of alcohol and other drugs may precipitate manic and depressive episodes in some people. The following are some drugs that may lower lithium blood levels:

- Aminophylline
- Caffeine
- Sodium bicarbonate
- Theophylline

Q: Is it possible to have a manic or depressive episode while taking full doses of lithium?

A: While lithium decreases the frequency, duration and severity of episodes of mood disorders, it does not necessarily totally eliminate episodes of depression or mania. About one third of bipolar patients taking lithium will never have other episodes.

Q: Is pregnancy safe while taking lithium?

A: There is good evidence that lithium can cause serious heart defects in babies born to mothers who take it during their first 3 months of pregnancy. About 1 in 1000 babies of mothers who took lithium during the first trimester were born with malformed hearts. Similar malformations develop in only 1 of 37,000 babies born to mothers who did not take lithium during their pregnancies.

Q: For nearly 15 years I have taken lithium and have been free from manic or depressive episodes. Because I was thinking of getting pregnant, I recently stopped taking lithium, but I became manic within 4 weeks. What are my options if I still want to become pregnant?

A: There are several possible ways to proceed:

1. Remain on lithium throughout the pregnancy and have your obstetrician use ultrasound and fetal echocardiography to detect possible heart malformations in the fetus. Remember that the chances of a congenital malformation are 1 in 1000.
2. Go off lithium a month prior to conceiving and restart the lithium in the fourth or fifth month of pregnancy.
3. Substitute clonazepam for lithium.
4. Take no medication throughout the pregnancy. If you

have an episode of severe mania or depression, plan with your psychiatrist that it will be treated with electroconvulsive therapy.

It is important that you discuss the advantages and disadvantages of each of these approaches with your psychiatrist and obstetrician.

Q: After discussing the risks and benefits, my doctors and I have decided that I will remain on lithium throughout my pregnancy. Are there any efforts that I can take to make my pregnancy safer?

A: If you are going to take lithium throughout your pregnancy you should make sure that you take the lowest possible dose, that you take it several times a day (not just once or twice) and that you drink plenty of fluids. Because the kidneys do not excrete much lithium around the time of delivery, you should stop the lithium 3 days prior to the expected date of delivery. It is important that you restart the lithium 3 days after delivery to help prevent a postpartum depression.

Q: I have been taking lithium for 8 years but recently stopped while pregnant. If I go back on lithium after I give birth, will it be safe for me to breast-feed my baby?

A: The concentration of lithium that is in breast milk is about one half of the amount of lithium that is in the mother's blood. Women on lithium should *not* nurse their babies.

Q: Is it safe for a man to father a child while taking lithium? Will the fact that I take lithium make it more difficult for my wife to get pregnant?

A: There is no evidence of danger to the fetus from a father who is taking lithium. Lithium should not make it difficult for you to impregnate your wife.

Q: My psychiatrist wants me to start taking lithium because of frequent cyclothymic mood swings. I've heard so much about the side effects of lithium that I am hesitant to take the drug. Can you tell me what the side effects are?

A: The chief side effects of lithium may be summarized as follows: increased thirst is experienced by 35 percent of all people taking lithium; 30 percent have increased urination and memory problems; 25 percent have tremors; 20 percent have weight gain; and 10 percent experience drowsiness and diarrhea.

Q: Which side effects do patients find most disturbing?

A: Patients who had stopped lithium against medical advice were asked which side effects played an important role in their decision to stop taking the drug. Thirty-five percent said it was the memory problems; 30 percent said the incoordination/tremors, weight gain and dulling of senses; 25 percent said the blurred vision, tiredness and lethargy, nausea and vomiting; and 20 percent said it was the excessive urination that made them stop.

Q: My doctor tells me that the lithium I have been taking for the past 3 years has reduced the activity of my thyroid gland. I am now taking thyroid hormone to correct this situation. Am I likely to have side effects from the thyroid medication?

A: Lithium will at times reduce the amount of thyroid hormone produced by the thyroid gland. When this happens the missing thyroid hormone can be replaced by thyroid tablets, which, when properly administered, should have no side effects.

Q: Since taking lithium, I have developed noticeable acne. What can I do to improve my skin?

A: Besides the usual dermatologic treatment of acne, many patients find that taking 50 mg of vitamin B_6 (pyridoxine) and 50 mg of zinc twice a day can be helpful. Acne usually takes several months to respond to treatment.

Q: Is it true that lithium reduces sex drive and performance?

A: Hypomania and mania often cause an increased sex drive. When taking lithium, some patients miss the increased sexuality associated with their periods of elevated mood. Otherwise, lithium seldom decreases sexual desire or the ability to enjoy sex.

Q: Since taking lithium, I have been passing large amounts of urine. Is there anything that can be done to reduce this annoying symptom?

A: There are several things that you can do. It may help to lower the dose of lithium, if possible. Also, taking lithium once rather than several times a day is often helpful. If neither of these measures help, you might ask your doctor about taking a diuretic. This may seem paradoxical, but for people taking lithium, diuretics cause a decrease rather than an increase in urine volume. Because diuretics usually result in increased lithium blood levels, expect your doctor to lower your lithium dose and to order frequent lithium blood tests after starting you on a diuretic. It is most important that you do not try to control your frequent urination by reducing the amount of liquid you drink! Since lithium makes you excrete a large amount of water, if you do not replace the water, you run the risk of becoming seriously dehydrated.

Q: My mother takes lithium and has become very forgetful. Is this due to the lithium or is she becoming senile?

A: Between one third and one quarter of the people who take lithium report memory problems. For some, this problem is minor, but others find it very embarrassing. Some experts believe that high-potency B vitamins plus folic acid supplementation may combat memory loss. However, high doses of vitamin B_6 often cause neurological symptoms and you should therefore consult your mother's physician before starting her on a program of vitamin supplementation.

Q: I take lithium and it seems to make me gain weight. Is there any solution to this problem?

A: By sticking to a calorie-restricted diet (such as the one promoted by Weight Watchers, for example) it is indeed possible to lose weight while taking lithium. Also, if excessive urination from lithium makes you thirsty, be careful not to quench your thirst by drinking fruit juices or sodas that are high in calories.

Q: Is it safe to stay on lithium for many years?

A: Some people have now taken lithium for over 30 years. There does not seem to be any relationship between long-term lithium treatment and the possibility of developing serious illnesses such as heart disease or cancer. However, some individuals taking lithium develop permanently reduced thyroid function and have to take thyroid hormone. It was once thought that lithium was likely to cause damage to the kidneys, but experience over many years shows that this happens only rarely.

Q: I have had only one manic episode in my life. Do I have to stay on lithium for the rest of my life?

A: Whether someone should take lithium indefinitely depends on several factors. People who have severe manic episodes and those whose social, family, or occupational situations would be seriously harmed if they had another manic episode, probably should take lithium indefinitely. After many years of successful lithium treatment, some patients choose to cease taking their lithium and studies show that many people have a manic episode within 6 months of stopping. For reasons that are poorly understood, when such people resume lithium treatment, the lithium sometimes fails to work as well as it did initially.

Q: I have a relative with bipolar disorder who keeps going off his medications. Each time he stops, he has a severe manic or depressive episode that puts him in the hospital. Why does he keep stopping a drug that clearly helps him?

A: There are several reasons why people stop lithium: they are unwilling to tolerate the side effects; they would rather feel manic or hypomanic than "normal"; they don't like being reminded that they have a problem by having to take medications; or they dislike the idea of being "dependent" or "controlled" by a medication.

LITHIUM SUBSTITUTES

Q: I am bipolar and lithium does not control my manic or depressive episodes. What are other possible drug treatments?

A: Over the last 20 years it has become clear that drugs other than lithium may be useful in controlling mood swings. The major drugs that are used with lithium, or in its place, are Tegretol and Depakote, which were used for many years as anticonvulsants and were then shown to work for mood swings as well. While these drugs are frequently used in the treatment of bipolar depressions, they are sometimes useful for treating unipolar depressions that have not responded to usual treatments.

Q: I am taking Tegretol and my doctor wants me to have frequent blood tests. I thought blood tests were used only for lithium.

A: A different type of blood test is used for Tegretol. In approximately 1 in 150,000 people, Tegretol causes changes in bone marrow. Bone marrow produces blood and any suppression may lead to a decrease in various blood cells. If this marrow inactivity is recognized early, treatment will prevent serious consequences or even death. Frequent blood tests, especially in the early stages of Tegretol treatment, are also needed to see if there are any cell changes. Also, blood levels for Tegretol are sometimes measured to determine the correct dosage of Tegretol.

Q: What are the side effects of Tegretol?

A: Some of the common side effects of Tegretol and the percentage of people who experience them are as follows: dizziness and unsteadiness is experienced by 20 percent; 15 percent experience rash; and 10 percent experience nausea, drowsiness and blurred or double vision.

Q: I am often in a mixed state, I have depressive and manic symptoms simultaneously and am currently taking Tofranil and lithium. I was referred to a psychopharmacologist who wants me
to stop both of those drugs and replace them with Tegretol. Why
does he want me to do this?

A: Antidepressants sometimes cause or perpetuate mixed states.
At times this happens despite the administration of lithium.
Many patients bothered by mixed states do well when treated
with Tegretol or Depakote, sometimes in conjunction with lithium. A few patients with severe mixed states only respond to
lithium combined with both Depakote and Tegretol. After starting Tegretol, better sleep probably will be the first improvement
you will notice. Other symptoms of mania usually improve next
and depressive symptoms generally are the last to be controlled.

Q: Because my daughter had a manic episode that did not respond
to lithium, she is now in the hospital. She has been on Tegretol
for the past month and has shown little response. Her doctor
says that we should be patient and give the medication a chance.
For someone having a manic episode, how long should one
continue Tegretol before deciding that it is not effective?

A: If Tegretol is not effective in controlling mania after 3 weeks at
a therapeutic blood level, it is unlikely to become effective.

Q: My doctor wants to prescribe Depakote for my rapid cycling
bipolar disorder. What side effects might I expect if I were to take
this drug?

A: Some common side effects of Depakote and the percentage of
people who experience them are: loss of appetite, nausea and
vomiting—15 percent; and rash, hair loss, weakness/fatigue,
headache and sedation/drowsiness—5 percent.

Q: My doctor has prescribed Tegretol along with an antidepressant.
Don't these drugs work against each other and cancel each
other's actions?

A: When there is a possibility that an antidepressant may cause mania, a major mood regulating drug (lithium, Tegretol or Depakote) is often prescribed along with the antidepressant. The two drugs work together and do not neutralize each other.

Q: My doctor wants to start me on Depakote for treatment of episodes of mania and depression that lithium has not prevented. Is this a standard treatment?

A: When someone with bipolar disorder does not respond to lithium, either Depakote or Tegretol will frequently bring the mood swings under control. The combination of drugs is worth a try if lithium alone has failed.

Q: Why are large doses of thyroid medication prescribed for some people with bipolar illness?

A: High doses of thyroid medications can slow down the cycling process in some people with rapid cycling bipolar disorder. There is a close connection between thyroid function and the cycling process. Anyone whose moods cycle frequently should have a complete thyroid evaluation that includes a panel of blood tests. If your thyroid is going to be evaluated, make sure the doctor orders a test of thyroid stimulating hormone, also known as a TSH test. This test often detects thyroid problems well before they show up on routine tests.

Q: My sister is in the hospital with a manic episode that has not responded to lithium, Tegretol or several other treatments. Her doctor has mentioned starting her on verapamil. What is verapamil and is it likely to help?

A: Verapamil belongs to a group of medications known as calcium-channel blockers. Many psychopharmacologists find that verapamil and other calcium-channel blockers are effective against mania when other medications do not help. Verapamil has also been used as prophylactic drug to control rapid cycling bipolar disorder. (Don't be surprised if you hear of people taking verapamil for heart disease, for this is in fact the most common use of the drug.)

Q: I have been having seven or eight episodes of mania and depression each year for some time. I have taken lithium, Tegretol and Depakote at various times. None of these drugs reduced the number or severity of episodes. What else might be done to control my mood swings?

A: Some rapid cycling bipolar patients do not respond to lithium, Tegretol or Depakote when taken individually. Some patients must take all three drugs simultaneously; the combination often creates a synergistic effect and improvement occurs. Large doses of thyroid hormones may also be useful.

ANTIPSYCHOTICS

Q: What is an antipsychotic drug?

A: Antipsychotic drugs are medications that control psychotic symptoms sometimes seen in schizophrenia and major affective disorders.

Q: Other than for a severe manic episode, when might antipsychotic medications be appropriately prescribed for people with mood disorders?

A: Other situations in which antipsychotics may be useful are when someone is having a psychotic depression or suffering with schizoaffective disorder. There are some people with treatment-resistant nonpsychotic depressions who will only respond to antidepressants when small doses of antipsychotics are added to their other medications.

Q: Why are antipsychotic drugs such as Haldol or Stelazine sometimes prescribed along with lithium? Do they have antidepressant or antimanic effects as well?

A: Antipsychotic drugs sometimes are used along with lithium during depressive or manic episodes that are characterized by severe hyperactivity or psychotic symptoms (such as delusions or hallucinations). These drugs will shorten the length of time the patient remains overactive and/or psychotic, but they will not affect the episode itself. Because of the possibility of causing severe permanent involuntary movements (tardive dyskinesia), the use of antipsychotics should be as brief as possible. Some patients with schizoaffective disorder may require long-term treatment with the combination of lithium and an antipsychotic drug.

Q: When I was hospitalized with a manic episode I was given both lithium and Haldol. In the past I was given just lithium. Why the change?

A: Lithium alone often helps people with mild or moderately severe manic episodes. Patients who are having very severe mania may require relief faster than the 10 to 14 days that lithium usually takes to be effective. Haldol and other antipsychotic medications often provide fast relief from severe mania.

Q: Do antipsychotic drugs cause many serious side effects?

A: The most disturbing side effects of antipsychotics are the various bodily movement disorders that they cause. Involuntary movements of the tongue, neck, limbs or eyes—dystonic movements— are common, especially during the first weeks of treatment. Tremors, slowed movements and pseudoparkinsonism are possible as well. Another very disturbing side effect that some people experience is an inner sense of restlessness, called akathisia. Akathisia generally is most severe during the third month of taking antipsychotics. These side effects often may be controlled by using antiparkinsonian drugs or Inderal. Other side effects of antipsychotics include dry mouth, drowsiness, lowered blood pressure, constipation, blurred vision and weight gain.

ELECTROCONVULSIVE THERAPY (ECT)

Q: What is shock treatment and when is it used?

A: Shock treatment is a form of treatment in which an electric current is briefly passed through the brain. The purpose of the electricity is to induce the same sort of brain wave changes that occur during a generalized convulsion. ECT is most often used to treat severe depressions. It is also used for the treatment of episodes of severe mania. ECT can be life-saving and is often effective when other forms of treatment have failed.

Q: What exactly happens when someone gets shock treatment?

A: The patient must first give informed consent for having ECT. The psychiatrist must explain to the patient the expected benefits of this form of treatment, its alternatives and possible side effects. The patient is encouraged to ask questions about the procedure and its results and side effects, and he should expect detailed answers. The patient also should be informed that he may withdraw consent at any time, and in the event that this happens, treatments will be stopped. Prior to the first treatment, the patient should have a physical examination, a chest x-ray, an electrocardiogram and blood and urine tests. The patient should take nothing by mouth for 6 hours before ECT and should void immediately prior to the treatment. An intravenous infusion is started and medications are administered to reduce saliva, induce sleep and to relax the muscles of the body. Once the medications are fully effective, the actual electrical stimulus, delivered through electrodes, is applied to the head. The electrical stimulus produces brain wave changes that are characteristic of a seizure and it is believed that it is this seizure that has a beneficial effect on mood disorders. After the treatment patients may sleep for about 30 minutes. They will often awake in a somewhat confused state. When fully awake the patient may have breakfast, and if the treatments are being done on an outpatient basis, the patient may then return home.

Q: Does ECT cause brain damage?

A: There is no evidence that shock treatments cause brain damage. In a recent study of depressed patients who received more than 100 treatments, psychological testing showed that memory and other mental functions were the same in the group of patients who never received ECT. Another recent study using magnetic resonance imaging (MRI) did not detect any evidence that ECT caused any structural changes in the brain.

Q: My father's psychiatrist wants to administer ECT to him because his depression has been resistant to treatment with a variety of medications. Isn't ECT a controversial treatment?

A: The controversy surrounding ECT has little to do with therapeutic merit and, in my opinion, is political in nature. Like the use of Ritalin for treating children with attention problems, and Prozac for treating depression, ECT has been the target of negative propaganda that originated with the anti-psychiatry movement. ECT plays an important role in the treatment of depression throughout the world.

Q: My psychiatrist wants me to have ECT, but I am afraid. Just how dangerous is it?

A: ECT is administered with anesthesia and muscle-relaxing drugs and it is a safe procedure. In one study, 99,425 ECT treatments were given to 18,627 patients. In that series there were only two deaths. In comparison, the death rate from childbirth is six times as high.

Q: How do patients treated with ECT rate the treatments?

A: In a study of nearly 200 people who were treated with ECT, about 80 percent reported being helped by the treatments, about 75 percent considered the treatments no more frightening than going to the dentist and 13 percent indicated that they would be reluctant to have ECT again.

Q: While I can understand how antidepressants work, none of my doctors have been able to explain to me how ECT works. Are they deliberately avoiding the question?

A: The fact is that no one knows exactly how ECT reduces depression. Many believe that it is likely that ECT has the same effects on neurotransmitters and their receptors in the brain as do antidepressants and this produces the improvement.

Q: Will I have to be hospitalized to receive ECT?

A: ECT may be safely administered to both inpatients and outpatients. On an outpatient basis, the treatments may be given either in a hospital clinic or in a psychiatrist's office. It is important that outpatients be accompanied to and from the treatments by a responsible person. Many people have ECT done on an outpatient basis, thereby avoiding hospitalization.

Q: My doctor talks about unilateral and bilateral ECT. What does she mean by these terms?

A: Bilateral ECT refers to a type of treatment where electrodes are applied to both sides of the head, while in unilateral treatments the electrodes are applied to only one side of the head. Many psychiatrists believe that unilateral treatments have the advantage of producing less memory loss than bilateral treatments, but unilateral treatments seem to be somewhat less effective than bilateral ECT. Depressed patients who do not respond to unilateral treatments usually get over their depressions when treated bilaterally.

Q: How often are shock treatments given?

A: Physicians trained in the United States usually administer three treatments a week, while those trained in England and some other countries usually treat their patients twice a week. Although the end results are the same, patients treated three times a week generally recover from their depressions somewhat more rapidly.

Q: My son, who is severely depressed and suicidal, will be starting an ECT series. How many treatments is he likely to receive and how will his doctor know when to stop giving him this treatment?

A: ECT is given until the patient's mood, thinking and behavior have improved. Most people require between eight and ten treatments to obtain maximal improvement from ECT, but the exact number of treatments will vary from person to person.

Treatments are stopped when the psychiatrist notices that the patient's depression has greatly improved.

Q: I have taken lithium for many years and it has done a good job of preventing episodes of mania. I have recently become severely depressed and my depression has not responded to intense treatment with two antidepressants. My psychiatrist is worried about my suicidal preoccupations, and has suggested that I stop my lithium and the antidepressant I am currently taking and have ECT. Why is it important that I stop the lithium?

A: Your psychiatrist has asked you to stop your lithium because ECT when administered to someone taking lithium often results in severe confusion and clouding of consciousness.

Q: My wife is going to have ECT at her psychiatrist's office. What will she be like when I take her home after a treatment?

A: Immediately following a treatment your wife probably will be a bit confused and it may take her a while to recognize that she is home. Because of the memory loss that follows a treatment she may be upset by not being able to find things around the house. She may need to be reminded that the memory loss is a temporary effect of the ECT and that her memory will return. Some people have a headache immediately following ECT. Simple remedies such as aspirin or Tylenol are usually effective for these headaches.

Q: I have had bipolar disorder for many years and because I am not very good about taking my lithium, I have had over a dozen hospitalizations. Two weeks into my last hospitalization for a severe psychotic episode, I was given ECT when I did not respond to medication. The shock treatments were effective in ending my manic episode. If I have another manic episode, will I require ECT again?

A: Severe manic episodes are potentially life-threatening and must be brought under control as rapidly as possible. When someone in a severe manic episode does not respond to medication, ECT is effective approximately 80 percent of the time. Generally, bilateral treatments are administered until the patient responds.

If the mania is extremely severe, a patient may be given more than the normal three treatments per week. It generally takes less than twenty treatments to bring about maximum improvement in a manic patient. If you will take your medication regularly it will prevent future episodes. If you have manic episodes despite the lithium and drug treatment is started at the earliest indication of the onset of another episode, you probably will not need ECT.

Q: A week ago, my mother finished a series of eight ECTs for the treatment of a severe depression. She is now depression-free, but she is having problems with her memory. Will her memory ever be normal again?

A: Almost all people who receive ECT have temporary memory problems during the series of treatments and for a period of time after the last treatment. Sometimes it takes 2 or 3 months for the memory to return to normal. Some events that occurred near the time of the treatments may never be remembered.

Q: How long do the beneficial effects of ECT last?

A: When patients respond to a course of ECT by recovering from depression, it is important that they start taking an antidepressant. Patients who do not take antidepressants have approximately a 50 percent chance of relapse in the 6 months following ECT.

Q: My doctor tells me that I have "treatment-resistant depression." I have been on many antidepressants by themselves and in various combinations. At times I took lithium with antidepressants. None of these treatments have helped me feel better. My psychiatrist has suggested that I have an ECT series. Is ECT likely to help?

A: While ECT is effective in about 80 percent of patients treated early in the course of their depression, it is effective about 50 percent of the time in those whose depressions have been resistant to adequate treatment with many antidepressants.

Q: My severe depression has not responded to treatment with many antidepressants, but I have recently had a good response to ECT. My doctor now wants to give me ECT every 3 or 4 weeks to prevent me from becoming depressed again. Is this a recognized form of treatment?

A: Some people who do not respond to antidepressants may remain depression-free with maintenance ECT. Maintenance ECT is shock treatment every 3 to 6 weeks. In rare instances, maintenance ECT may be continued for years.

PSYCHOSURGERY

Q: My brother has had severe depression for many years and has not responded to various treatments. It has been suggested that he seek psychosurgery. What is it?

A: Psychosurgery is brain surgery designed to improve severe psychiatric disorders. Two types of brain surgery, called cingulotomy and stereotactic subcaudate tractotomy, are often effective for those people with mood disorders for whom all other methods of treatment have failed. Cingulotomies have helped about 70 percent of patients with severe unipolar or bipolar depressions. About one half of those treated with stereotactic subcaudate tractotomy were helped by that procedure. Psychosurgical techniques are used more frequently in England than in the United States.

Q: Are these procedures like lobotomies?

A: These new techniques are similar to lobotomies in that they both involve operations on the brain. However, they differ in the extent of surgery involved. Unlike lobotomies, modern psychosurgical techniques target specific parts of the brain involved in the regulation of mood. Lobotomies destroy much more brain tissue than cingulotomy or subcaudate tractotomy.

Q: I have not responded to three antidepressants. Does this mean
         that I will need psychotherapy?

A: Psychosurgery is suggested very rarely. Almost all people who
         have not responded to even three different antidepressants will
         improve without the need for any type of brain surgery. Either
         more intensive antidepressant therapy or ECT will usually be
         enough to control their depressions.

SECTION 3

Special Aspects of Mood Disorders

CHILDREN AND ADOLESCENTS

Q: Do very young children become depressed?

A: Yes, in fact, depression may even be present in infants. Depressed infants appear lethargic and are often severely underweight due to the fact that they nurse poorly. Sometimes depression is the reason that some infants seem not to "thrive." In a recent study of preschool children, 8 percent were diagnosed as being depressed.

Q: How common is depression in elementary and high school students?

A: Studies of children in these grades have found that approximately 15 to 20 percent were depressed.

Q: How do you recognize a depressed child or adolescent?

A: Depression among children usually appears differently than it does in adults. Irritability, anxiety and complaints of boredom are often indicators that a child or adolescent is depressed. The following is a list of some ways in which depression might show itself:

- Decreased school performance
- Accident proneness
- Concentration problems
- Social withdrawal
- Anxiety
- Decreased energy
- Excessive risk-taking behavior
- Sleep problems
- Loss of interest in friends
- Aggression
- Loss of interest in activities
- Low self-esteem
- Talking or reading about death
- Temper tantrums
- Sudden gain or loss of weight
- Irritability
- Neglect of appearance
- Alcohol or drug use
- Headaches, stomach and body aches
- Guilt feelings
- Suicidal thoughts
- Suicidal behavior

Q: Are there any indications that an adolescent may be suicidal?

A: Suicidal behavior in adolescents is more difficult to detect and predict than it is in adults. However, the possibility of suicide exists in any adolescent who shows one or several of the symptoms of depression listed above. Adolescents who openly verbalize their wish for death by saying things such as "I'd be better off dead," or who suddenly give away their valued possessions should be considered acutely suicidal and should have an emergency psychiatric evaluation immediately. These threats often turn out to be real.

Q: What are some of the things that predispose a child or adolescent to become depressed?

A: Among the factors that increase the likelihood that a child will become depressed are: one or more relatives who have a history of depression, a history of physical abuse, emotional maltreatment, a history of foster care or a history attention problems in school.

Q: How common is suicide in adolescents?

A: Suicide is the third leading cause of death among 15- to 19-year-olds. Only traffic accidents and homicides kill more teenagers than suicide does. Officially about 7000 teenagers kill themselves each year in the United States. The actual statistic is probably twice as high because many suicides are officially classified as accidental deaths.

Q: What can be done for a depressed child or adolescent?

A: Depressed children and adolescents should be evaluated by a psychiatrist familiar with the diagnosis and treatment of depression in this age group. It is a grave error to assume that a depression represents "a phase that will be outgrown." If there is a family history of depression, one should be especially on the lookout for depressive symptoms.

Q: I suspect that my adopted 17-year-old son may suffer from bipolar disorder. He mopes around his room for weeks, refusing to see his friends or even to talk to them on the phone. Then, for a month or so, he is full of life and gets overinvolved in social activities. In elementary school a psychologist diagnosed him as "hyperactive." Can bipolar disorder start as early as adolescence?

A: About 40 percent of people with bipolar disorder have the onset of their illness between the ages of 15 and 25. It is common for those with an early onset of bipolar disorder to have been diagnosed as "hyperactive" or as having attention deficit disorder (ADD) while in elementary school.

Q: Do young children kill themselves?

A: As incredible as it may sound, suicide has been an increasing cause of death in children and adolescents. Suicides have occurred in children as young as 4 years of age.

Q: My 16-year-old son recently was evaluated for depression at the outpatient department of a well-known hospital. Because of his normal dexamethasone suppression test (DST), the psychiatrist now doubts that my son is depressed. Is the DST so accurate that a diagnosis of depression can be based on it?

A: While the dexamethasone suppression test is often useful in confirming a diagnosis of depression, it is especially unreliable in adolescents. The diagnosis of depression is a clinical diagnosis and its existence should not be excluded because of negative laboratory results.

Q: My son has been depressed for the past 3 months. He refuses to see a psychologist or psychiatrist. Recently I have been fearful that he may be suicidal. Should I ask him directly if he is having suicidal thoughts?

A: Suicidal thinking is common in depressions. While many adults and teenagers who have suicidal thoughts may be reluctant to talk about them spontaneously, they are often relieved when asked about them and will usually be truthful about such thoughts. Therefore, yes, it can be useful to take the initiative and ask your son how he feels. If he is having suicidal thoughts you can get him the help he needs. Remember, a person with plans for suicide and the means to carry them out should not be left alone for a moment and an immediate psychiatric evaluation should be arranged.

Q: I worry about my daughter. She had a psychotic manic episode at age 17 and a severe depression at age 19. I also think she has started to drink heavily. Does someone with the onset of bipolar disorder in adolescence have a worse outcome than someone with a later onset of the illness?

A: There have been several studies in which the long-term outcome of people with the onset of bipolar disorder in adolescence was compared with the outcome of those who had the onset of the illness later in their lives. Results show that the course of the illness is much the same in both groups. Alcohol abuse is common in adolescents with mood disorders and reduces the beneficial effects of treatment. If your daughter stops abusing alcohol and receives adequate treatment, there is a good chance that she will have a happy and a productive life.

Q: My 9-year-old son has been diagnosed as having had a manic episode and has been started on lithium. I am surprised that he is taking the same amount of lithium that I take. Why is it that children seem to need such high doses of lithium?

A: There are two major reasons why children require lithium doses that seem to be high. Children's kidneys excrete lithium more efficiently than do adults' kidneys. This means that a relatively large dose is necessary to maintain adequate blood levels. It has also been observed that children frequently require higher blood levels of lithium to get maximum benefit from it.

THE ELDERLY

Q: Is depression common in older people?

A: Severe depression is uncommon among elderly persons who live in their own homes, as opposed to a nursing home, or other facility. Among a group of elderly people who were 65 years old or older, approximately 1.5 percent of the men and 4 percent of the women reported being depressed. Mild depressive symptoms were also reported by 27 percent of people over the age of 60. Depression is more common in women, in older people who are in poor health, in those who have experienced the death of a spouse, and in those older people who lack supportive family and friends. In nursing homes where the environment lacks stimulation, and where residents feel isolated and lonely, it is not surprising that nearly one-quarter of the residents are severely depressed. Untreated depression in nursing home residents is predictive of early death.

Q: My 78-year-old father has been depressed for a few months. Because his blood pressure is very high and hard to control, he sees his general practitioner once a month. Why doesn't his physician recognize that he is depressed and what should I do to help the situation?

A: Diagnosing depression in an older person may be difficult because some of the symptoms of depression such as poor sleep and appetite may also occur in the non-depressed aged. In older people, depressed moods may not be as noticeable as in younger people. Non-psychiatric physicians often fail to diagnose depression in their patients. This problem is especially prevalent when a physician's elderly patient has many physical disorders.

I suggest that you accompany your father the next time he goes to his doctor. This will give you an opportunity to describe the changes to his doctor that you have noted over the past few months that cause you to believe that your father is depressed. If the doctor still does nothing about the depression, you may want to arrange to have your father evaluated by a psychiatrist familiar with the problems of the elderly.

Q: My 75-year-old mother who has had many depressions has recently become manic for the first time in her life. Her psychiatrist wants to treat her with electroconvulsive therapy (ECT) and then start lithium to prevent mood swings in the future. Isn't she too old for ECT and lithium?

A: ECT is a highly effective treatment for people of all ages who are having manic episodes. Many people much older than your mother have been successfully treated with ECT for mood disorders. Children as young as 5 years old and even those in their 90s have had great success starting lithium therapy. Advanced age is in itself no reason to decide against lithium treatment. If your mother's heart and kidneys are functioning well, she should be able to take lithium safely. In the elderly, effective levels of lithium in the blood usually are often achieved with lower doses than those necessary with younger people.

Q: Are there special treatments for depressed older people?

A: Both antidepressant medications and ECT can be safely used with elderly patients. For severely depressed elderly patients, ECT is by far the most effective and probably the safest treatment. If antidepressants are prescribed, it is important that they initially be administered in smaller doses than those used for younger people. "Start low and go slow" is the rule physicians should follow when prescribing for older people. Elavil, Vivactil, Surmontil and Sinequan frequently cause confusion in older people and should therefore be avoided. Prozac and Zoloft are often very effective in older persons, especially when started in very low doses and they do not usually cause serious side effects.

Q: My 82-year-old grandmother is an extremely bright and intelligent woman. Gradually, she has started to become depressed and at these times her memory rapidly deteriorates and she becomes confused. What can we do to help her?

A: When older people become depressed, their symptoms are often similar to those associated with Alzheimer's disease. Their memory may become faulty and they may be unable to remember how to do many very routine tasks. When dealing with a depressed patient who is in this situation, it is important to provide a structured routine that is simple and does not change from day to day. Other useful measures are to protect them from potentially upsetting situations and try to help them avoid tasks or situations that would aggravate their memory problems. It is also important not to confront them with the fact that they are unable to function as they once had. To bring their shortcomings to their attention serves no purpose whatsoever; it will not help them to remember and will do nothing but cause unnecessary distress.

Q: I read someplace that the elderly have an especially high suicide rate. My father, who has always kept his feelings to himself, seems awfully sad lately and I am very concerned about what kind of thoughts he might be having. Is there any way to predict which people are especially at risk to kill themselves?

A: The suicide rate among the elderly is twice as high as the suicide rate of the rest of the population. Just as it is with younger people, suicide among the elderly is associated with depression, alcoholism, chronic medical illness and also having access to firearms. A suicidal crisis is often precipitated by increasing medical difficulties, widowhood, death of a friend or relative, living alone and anticipation of nursing home placement. It is very important that depressed people—young and old—do not have access to firearms. This is particularly true of elderly males, as 66 percent of the suicides in this group are committed by shooting.

Q: My grandfather has taken lithium for over 20 years with a record of near perfect control of his bipolar disease. He has recently developed Parkinson's disease and his psychiatrist wants to take him off lithium and substitute Tegretol. Does this change make sense after so many years of successful lithium treatment?

A: Lithium often worsens Parkinson's disease, while Tegretol does not. It is most probable that your grandfather's bipolar disorder will be well controlled by the Tegretol.

Q: My grandmother, who has Alzheimer's disease, seems particularly depressed. Is her depression part of the disease or could it be a separate problem that perhaps can be treated?

A: Most patients with Alzheimer's disease are not usually depressed, at least it is not a common symptom. When depression accompanies Alzheimer's disease, it should be treated because it often can be controlled. Monamine oxidase (MAO) inhibitors are both safe and effective in treating depressed people with Alzheimer's disease. Alzheimer's patients who are taking MAO inhibitors must have their food intake closely supervised because they cannot be relied upon to observe the dietary restrictions required by MAO therapy.

DEPRESSION AND BEREAVEMENT

Q: My mother-in-law died 5 months ago and my wife has been miserable ever since. How can I know if she is grieving the death or has developed a real depression beyond the sadness she feels over losing her mother? Do grief and depression have the same symptoms?

A: The symptoms of bereavement and depression have many similarities, but they are two distinctly different problems. Bereaved people may have many symptoms of depression during the first year of bereavement: crying, sleep disturbances, depressed mood, loss of appetite, fatigue, restlessness and poor memory are experienced by more than half of those who are bereaved.

One difference is that depressed moods usually occur in waves among bereaved people, compared to the constant symptoms that are usually experienced by those who are depressed. In a study of a group of bereaved individuals, 42 percent reported full depression at some point during the first year of bereavement, but by the end of the year, only 8 percent still felt depressed. Although 17 percent of this group reported seeing, hearing or feeling the presence of the deceased, such hallucinations are not a common symptom of severe mental illness and will usually disappear by the end of the first year. Some common depressive symptoms *never* occur in people with uncomplicated grief; delusions, suicide attempts, profound slowing of mental and locomotor functions and continuous severe guilt feelings were not seen in any of 149 bereaved individuals in a recent study. If your wife were to show any of these symptoms it would suggest that a depression has replaced her normal grieving process, in which case you should bring her to a psychiatrist.

Q: Does bereavement cause physical symptoms?

A: Bereaved individuals frequently experience a decrease in their feeling of well being and may develop physical symptoms. Among the symptoms reported are: dizziness, dysmenorrhea, headaches, fainting, nightmares, blurred vision, digestive problems, frequent urination, palpitations, chest pain, shortness of breath and muscle aches. In one study, widows and widowers were found to have four times as many hospitalizations as married people of the same age!

Q: What is meant by abnormal grief?

A: Some people show an absence of expected or normal grief. An individual who has just experienced the death of a significant other who shows no manifestations of grief, carries on with life as if nothing had happened and insists that she is "doing just fine" is very likely to be having a problem. It is normal to be sad and to show it; in fact it is considered by many to be unhealthy *not* to show such feelings and can possibly be the cause of many problems. If someone displays no evidence of grieving, they should be encouraged to see a psychotherapist skilled in the management of grief. For some individuals, what starts out as normal grief does not resolve and continues for an extended period; this can result in depression. Profound slowing of mental and physical processes—otherwise known as psychomotor retardation—is not part of normal grief and neither is suicidal thinking. Individuals who show these symptoms should immediately have a psychiatric evaluation. (Such individuals generally require both psychotherapy and antidepressant medication.) Another abnormal type of grief is profound denial, an example of which is the inability to throw away any of the dead person's clothing or possessions. Also, a bereaved person who shows frenetic activity accompanied by inappropriately cheerful moods is displaying abnormal grief. Bereaved individuals who show excessive, prolonged anger and hostility in response to their loss are also showing pathological grief.

Q: Is it possible to predict which bereaved individuals will have an especially hard time dealing with bereavement?

A: A good predictor that a person will go on to develop a long-standing chronic depression once they are bereaved is if they were in poor physical or mental health before the loss. Additional predictors are a history of drug or alcohol abuse.

Q: Do bereaved individuals require professional help?

A: Each year, approximately 85 percent of the 800,000 people in this country who are bereaved resolve their grief without professional help of any kind. Those who develop major depressions should be treated by a psychiatrist. Bereaved individuals who show prolonged or abnormal grief reactions should start psychotherapy with a therapist experienced in working with the bereaved.

Q: I have heard that widows and widowers have an increased death rate during the first year of bereavement. Is this also true for parents who have lost a child?

A: The fact that widowers have 40 percent more deaths than non-bereaved males is an extremely telling piece of information. The increased mortality of widowers results from an increase in deaths from heart attacks, infectious diseases, accidents and suicide (not necessarily in this order). Surprisingly, there is not a similar increase in deaths in widowed women, or in parents who have lost a child.

SUICIDE

Q: How common is suicide in the United States?

A: About one in every hundred deaths is the result of suicide. In the United States, about 30,000 deaths are officially ruled to be suicides. However, most experts believe that the actual number of completed suicides is about twice as high as that number because so many deaths actually caused by suicide are officially ruled as accidental.

Q: Do most people who kill themselves suffer from depression?

A: About 60 percent of those who kill themselves were depressed before their death. People with untreated or undertreated mood disorders have a 30- to 70-fold increased risk of killing themselves compared to the rest of the general population.

Q: Is there a relationship between the level of depression and suicide?

A: While it is true that most people who kill themselves were depressed prior to committing suicide, there is no simple relationship between the severity of depression and the likelihood of a suicide attempt. The best predictor of the possibility of a suicide attempt is the extent of hopelessness the person is experiencing. People feeling hopeless are more at risk for suicidal behavior than people who are optimistic about the future.

Q: I had a friend who was in severe pain from a cancer that had spread to her bones. Her excruciating pain was not controlled by medication and she was in constant pain. She ended up killing herself. Throughout her illness I visited her frequently and despite the terrible pain she had, she never complained of depression. It seems to me that she ended her life because she could no longer bear the pain she was in and that she knew it would never get better, but only worse. Would psychiatrists consider her suicide to be a rational act?

A: The possibility that people who are not depressed may rationally decide to end their lives is a topic of heated debate, especially with the recent increase in "assisted" suicides, especially those involving physicians. Many psychiatrists believe that the decision to take one's life is never a rational decision, but many psychiatrists—myself included—believe that under certain unusual circumstances individuals may rationally decide to end their lives for reasons that have nothing to do with depression. When a depressed person commits suicide, it cannot be considered a rational act, even when it makes perfect sense to the person performing the act; the decision to end one's life is almost always the product of profound hopelessness.

Q: Is it true that those who talk openly about suicide do not follow through?

A: The belief that people who talk about suicide never kill themselves is a most dangerous myth. Of course not everyone who talks about suicide will actually carry it out, but studies show that close to 80 percent of those who did commit suicide talked openly about the subject in the days and weeks prior to their deaths. Apparently, physicians often do not recognize suicidal patients; in one study approximately one half the people who killed themselves had seen their physicians in the month prior to their suicides. What may seem to be a mere passing mention of suicide should always be taken with the utmost seriousness and an immediate psychiatric evaluation should be scheduled.

Q: Is it dangerous for me—a social worker—to come right out and confront my depressed clients about whether or not they are considering suicide? If they have not considered suicide, I would hate to think of putting the idea into their head.

A: Almost everyone who is severely depressed has thought of suicide at some point. However, thinking or talking about it and actually carrying it out are two very different things. There is no risk that you might promote suicide by asking depressed persons if they have thought about killing themselves. In fact, it is an important question to ask in determining whether a person is contemplating suicide.

Q: Which people are at the greatest risk for suicide?

A: There are some characteristics and situations that increase the possibility of suicide. Among these are: being in a mixed state (showing manic and depressive symptoms simultaneously); having delusions or hallucinations; a history of ongoing drug or alcohol abuse; severe anxiety or panic attacks accompanied by depression; and having an impulsive, irritable or angry temperament.

Q: In addition to psychological factors, what other social or situational characteristics help identify suicidal individuals?

A: A majority of demographic studies have shown that people with the following characteristics are at greater risk for suicide:

- Living alone
- Ill health
- Depression
- A recent loss
- Becoming unemployed

- A history of sexual abuse
- Being a white male
- Social isolation
- Being divorced
- Having access to firearms

Q: My father is a hunter and has many guns in his house. He has recently become extremely depressed and as a precaution we have asked him to give up his guns, but he refuses. Is our concern well-founded?

A: Yes. Firearms are the number one method of suicide in the United States. Self-inflicted gunshot wounds kill more people than all other methods of suicide combined. The risk that someone who owns a gun will commit suicide is 4.8 times greater than someone who does not own one.

Q: Can psychiatric treatment reduce the chance that someone will commit suicide?

A: Research shows that the treatment of depression and the use of long-term medication to prevent episodes of depression reduce the number of suicides. Both adequate psychopharmacologic treatment and electroconvulsive therapy can reduce the risk of suicide. Adequate treatment of mood disorders is suicide prevention at its best. Several studies of people with bipolar disorder, before and after taking lithium, have shown markedly decreased incidence of suicidal behavior after taking lithium.

Q: My husband is coming out of a severe depression. I would have thought that this would make him feel better, but his psychiatrist told me that there is actually an *increased* risk that he will commit suicide. Why is this?

A: Depression is often accompanied by feelings of great despair and hopelessness and a strong suicidal drive. Although depressed persons may have plans to kill themselves, they usually do not have the energy to carry them out. With someone like your husband, as his depression lifts, he could experience an increase in energy before there is any change in his feelings of hopelessness. For this reason, his risk of suicide is higher—not lower—than would be expected.

Q: Is it true that suicide is more likely to occur at certain times of the year?

A: Yes. There is a clustering of suicides in both the spring and the fall. April, May, June and October are months that have shown increases in the rate of suicide.

Q: Do suicidal tendencies run in families?

A: Until recently psychiatrists believed that there was no genetic predisposition toward suicide. Researchers have recently discovered that there are some families in which a tendency toward non-suicidal depression is passed down from generation to generation. In other families a tendency toward depression and suicide is transmitted. Additional evidence that a tendency toward suicidal behavior might be inherited comes from the study of twins. If one of a pair of identical twins kills herself, there is a one-in-five chance that the other twin will commit suicide. For non-identical twins the probability is zero.

DEPRESSION AND SEXUALITY

Q: Since becoming depressed I have almost totally lost interest in sex. Will my sex drive ever return?

A: One of the common symptoms of depression is loss of interest in many aspects of life, including sex. Sometimes losing interest in sex is the first symptom of depression. As your depression clears however your sexual interest should return.

Q: I've heard that frequent sexual activity can cause mania. Is this true?

A: There is no evidence that frequent sexual activity causes mania. It is often believed that mania is associated with increased sexuality and that increased sexual interest may be an early symptom of an oncoming manic episode, but this is simply not true.

SUBSTANCE ABUSE AND DEPRESSION

Q: My brother suffers from severe depression. We have recently discovered that he uses cocaine. Is it possible that his drug use is a result of his depression?

A: It is possible. The emotional pain resulting from depression may be so intolerable that people with depression turn to the temporary relief provided by the use of alcohol and other drugs. While in general, most people with depressions do not become dependent on drugs, those with mood disorders are at an increased risk of developing a drug or alcohol problem.

Q: Is there a relationship between depression and alcoholism?

A: The relationship between alcoholism and mood disorders is complex. People with mood disorders are two to three times as likely as the rest of the population to abuse alcohol and other drugs. Although some experts disagree, the mood disorder usually precedes the alcohol or drug abuse. As just mentioned, when people are depressed they often drink in an attempt to relieve their depression and, similarly, those with bipolar disease often use alcohol and other drugs in an attempt to induce manic-like feelings. However, what these people may not realize is that alcoholism and other forms of substance abuse can make the symptoms of a mood disorder more severe and resistant to treatment. Substance abuse of any type increases the risk of suicide in people with mood disorders.

Q: Does normal drinking make depression worse?

A: If by normal drinking you mean an occasional one or two drinks, there is no evidence that this amount of drinking will worsen the mood of a depressed person. Of course, people with severe alcohol abuse problems should not drink even this amount.

Q: My brother was recently admitted to a hospital for treatment of his alcoholism. He has been in the hospital for about 10 days. He told me that he is extremely depressed but the doctors at the hospital do not consider him a candidate for antidepressants. Why aren't they treating his depression?

A: During the first weeks of hospitalization for withdrawal from alcohol, many people appear to be severely depressed, but doctors do not usually respond right away. After 3 or 4 weeks in the hospital most of the depressions clear up by themselves. If the depression is severe and persists for more than 30 days, antidepressants should be considered at that time.

Q: Should I consider the advice from the people in my AA group? They say that I should stop taking lithium and antidepressants even though they help me so much? (I know from past experience that every time I stop my lithium, I became suicidal within a few weeks.) Apparently, my group is against all drug-taking, regardless of what the drug is or why it is being taken.

A: The official position of Alcoholics Anonymous is that "No AA member plays doctor." Often people in support groups offer advice that is not sound and inappropriate advice given to depressed alcoholics such as that they should stop taking their medications, has caused disastrous repercussions—even suicide. Many individual groups ignore the official position of AA and have taken irrational positions against the use of antidepressants and lithium. If the members of your AA group do not understand your need to take lithium and antidepressants, you may want to seek out an AA or Rational Recovery group that accepts the use of properly prescribed medications.

MOOD DISORDERS AND MEDICAL ILLNESSES

Q: Is it possible that my depression is caused by the medical problems I have?

A: Medical illnesses can cause mood changes. When a medical illness causes depression, there are usually symptoms of the underlying problem in addition to the symptoms of depression. Occasionally, depression is the first symptom of the illness and the picture does not become clear until other symptoms develop or laboratory test results suggest the true diagnosis. The following is a list of illnesses that can cause mood disorders:

Neurologic Diseases
- Alzheimer's disease and other dementias
- Brain tumors
- Encephalitis
- Epilepsy
- Huntington's disease
- Multiple sclerosis
- Narcolepsy
- Parkinson's disease
- Strokes
- Traumatic brain injury
- Wilson's disease

Hormonal-Metabolic Disorders
- Adrenal disorders
- Diabetes
- Ovarian failure
- Parathyroid disorders
- Pituitary disorders
- Porphyria
- Testicular failure
- Thyroid disorders

Infections
- AIDS
- Lyme disease
- Syphilis
- Viral illnesses (such as hepatitis)

Tumors
- Brain tumors
- Carcinoid tumors
- Cancer of the pancreas
- Pheochromocytoma

Toxins
- Addictive drugs (alcohol, heroin, etc.)
- Aluminum
- Arsenic
- Bismuth
- Carbon monoxide
- Lead
- Magnesium
- Manganese
- Mercury
- Organophosphate insecticides
- Thallium
- Zinc

Q: My mother developed a severe depression after having a stroke. Is this type of depression treatable?

A: In a recent study, approximately one quarter of the patients who suffered a stroke subsequently developed a major depression. The depression that follows a stroke is not simply a reaction to enormous emotional changes that the stroke may have caused; in many persons the depression is a direct result of brain damage caused by the stroke. (Depression is particularly likely in people who have had strokes involving the front of the left hemisphere of the brain.) It is crucial to realize that depression after a stroke is not simply a natural reaction to the fact that one has suddenly become disabled. If untreated these patients will still be depressed after 6 months. In depressed stroke patients, psychotherapy should be combined with either antidepressants or electroconvulsive therapy. Stroke patients who receive adequate treatment for their depression benefit more from rehabilitation than those whose depression remains untreated.

Q: My grandfather had a stroke and since then it seems as if he has developed Alzheimer's disease or at least something similar. He does not experience hardly any physical symptoms from the stroke, but he is apathetic, confused, forgetful and unable to take care of himself. Can a stroke cause dementia?

A: Especially in the elderly, it is possible for depression to cause pseudodementia, a condition in which people seem to have lost many mental functions such as memory and orientation. Pseudodementia is frequently the result of depression and treating the depression often helps restore the patient's former mental abilities. Your grandfather should have an expert evaluation for depression, as post-stroke depression often leads to pseudodementia. It is also possible that his mental deterioration is the direct result of brain damage that can be caused from having repeated small strokes.

Q: I have multiple sclerosis and every few years I have a relapse that is treated with intravenous steroids. I become very high while the steroids are being administered. I then crash into a depression. Is there anything that I can do to stabilize my moods when I get these cortisone treatments?

A: Steroids are among the drugs that can cause either manic or depressive symptoms. The effects of steroids on mood may be prevented by starting to take lithium 1 week or so before the steroids are administered and continuing for at least a month after they are discontinued.

Q: My aunt has had multiple sclerosis (MS) for many years. My last visit with her was very disturbing; while watching television, she would laugh and then suddenly cry, for no apparent reason. At times her emotional reactions would be to simple situations in commercials. What sort of mood disorder does she have and can anything be done to control it?

A: Some people with multiple sclerosis have difficulties regulating their expression of mood. They may laugh or cry in reaction to situations that others do not find emotional. Often their true feelings are very different from their apparent emotional reactions. The easy weeping and laughing is a result of the effects of multiple sclerosis on the brain. Small doses of Elavil have been found to control these exaggerated emotional reactions.

Q: My brother was in a motorcycle accident and had a severe head injury. Ever since regaining consciousness he has been over-talkative and elated. He also has started talking about grandiose plans for the future. There is no history of mood disorder in our family and my brother was just fine up to the time of his accident. What can be done to help him?

A: In the same way that some stroke victims regain consciousness and find themselves in a depression, other people may regain consciousness after a head injury and be in a manic or depressed state. Manic states following head injury usually result from injury to the right hemisphere of the brain. Lithium, Tegretol or Depakote can often control this type of mania. If drug treatment fails, ECT may be useful.

Q: Three years ago I was diagnosed as having chronic fatigue syndrome (CFS). My doctor told me to rest as much as possible and prescribed many vitamins. A few months ago I moved to a new community and changed physicians. My new doctor started me on Wellbutrin and lithium as he considered my lack of energy as a symptom of depression. Within 2 weeks of starting these new medications I had more energy than I had in the previous 3 years. Is chronic fatigue syndrome usually a symp-tom of depression?

A: Chronic fatigue syndrome is a mysterious condition that is related to depression in at least two ways. First, chronic fatigue is one of the chief symptoms of depression for certain people. Second, a chronic viral infection may be responsible for some cases of chronic fatigue syndrome. Viral infections are capable of causing depression. Of course, being chronically fatigued and unable to do much also may lead to depression. Antidepressants help about one half of all people with chronic fatigue syndrome. Cognitive behavior psychotherapy has also been shown to be a highly effective treatment for some CFS sufferers.

Q: My sister has AIDS and is becoming increasingly depressed. She says that there is no point in her taking antidepressants because her depression is a normal reaction to a hopeless situation. Can her depression be helped?

A: AIDS nearly always affects the brain and its functioning. As in patients with strokes, the depression that people with AIDS experience may result from altered brain function, not just from their horrible situation. Patients with AIDS who become depressed often respond to psychotherapy and antidepressants or stimulants. Stimulants such as Dexedrine or Ritalin can markedly improve mental functioning in some AIDS patients.

Q: Why is it that every time I have the flu I feel depressed?

A: Many viral illnesses result in depression. Such depressions can occur after bouts of the flu, mononucleosis, hepatitis and viral pneumonia.

Q: A cardiologist strongly recommended that my husband consult a psychiatrist for the depression he is presently experiencing. Why is he so concerned about the depression?

A: In people with untreated severe depression there are nearly eight times as many deaths from heart disease as in non-depressed people. Although depression is usually not considered a lethal disease, it should be vigorously treated in patients with heart conditions. Several antidepressants can be used safely by depressed individuals with heart problems. In other cardiac patients electroconvulsive therapy is the safest treatment.

Q: I have epilepsy and Tegretol does a good job of controlling my seizures. Although things are going well at work and with my family, I have recently become depressed. Are there any antidepressants that I should avoid because of my epilepsy and seizures?

A: Anafranil, Ludiomil and Wellbutrin often increase the frequency of seizures. Of the available antidepressants,

Norpramin, Desyrel and MAO inhibitors probably are least likely to increase the frequency of your seizures.

Q: My father became depressed and a few months later developed Parkinson's disease. Did the depression cause the disease? How is depression treated in people with Parkinson's disease?

A: Depression is the first symptom of Parkinson's disease about 15 percent of the time. About half of those with Parkinson's disease will become depressed at some point in their illness. It is likely that your father's depression resulted from his Parkinson's disease rather than vice versa. Ascendin and lithium are two mood-regulating medications that worsen Parkinson's disease. Wellbutrin often reduces the symptoms of Parkinsonianism as it improves depression. When prescribed in large amounts, Eldepryl, an MAO inhibitor often used for the treatment of Parkinson's disease, also has antidepressant effects

Q: I have recently been diagnosed with cancer. I have had surgery and am now scheduled to begin chemotherapy. I have had episodes of depression for the past 30 years. Will chemotherapy bring on an episode of depression?

A: Many drugs used to treat patients with cancer can induce mood changes. Among those that cause depression in some people are L-asparaginase, amphotericin B, interferon, methotrexate, procarbazine, tamoxifen, vinblastine and vincristine. Cortisone often causes both depression and mania. As with steroids used to treat multiple sclerosis, steroid-induced mood swings can be prevented by taking lithium prior to the start of the steroid treatment. Cooperation between a psychopharmacologist and an oncologist should allow cancer chemotherapy to proceed smoothly.

Q: How are mood disorders treated in patients with advanced cancer?

A: Psychotherapy helps many people to better adjust to having cancer. Antidepressants and ECT can be effective treatments for depressed cancer patients. Stimulants such as Ritalin or Dexedrine often give people with cancer increased energy. They can also reverse some of the mental clouding caused by narcotics and increase their pain-relieving actions.

MOOD DISORDERS AND THE LAW

Q: I am returning to work after a 6-week absence due to a severe depression. While I am sure I can carry out the responsibilities of my job, my medications impair my memory. Can my boss fire me if I have to write things down or use a tape recorder to remember things?

A: Under the recently implemented Americans with Disabilities Act (ADA), your employers may not fire workers if they can perform the "essential functions" of employment. Employers are required to make "reasonable accommodations" for people with disabilities to be able to work. Drug-induced memory impairments are considered to be a disability under ADA. Reasonable accommodations can include job restructuring, part-time or modified work schedules, reassignment to a vacant position, acquisition or modification of equipment or devices, the provision of readers or interpreters, or removal of barriers to access. Providing you with a tape recorder to augment your memory seems to be a reasonable accommodation. If you are fired, you may want to talk to a lawyer experienced with initiating a lawsuit under ADA.

Q: What aspects of employment are covered under the Americans with Disabilities Act?

A: The act covers all essential functions of employment including: recruitment, application procedures, hiring, upgrading, promotion, award of tenure, transfer, layoff, terminations, rehiring, compensation, job descriptions, leaves of absence, sick leave, fringe benefits, training and attendance at meetings and conferences.

Q: I have been severely depressed for the past 2 years. My lack of
         concentration has been so severe that I could not gather the
         financial data my accountant needed to prepare my income tax
         returns. Will the IRS accept my depression as a valid excuse for
         filing late and excuse me from the penalties for late filing?

A: On occasion the IRS has accepted medical information regard-
         ing depression as a valid excuse for late filing of tax returns late.
         Your lawyer should be consulted regarding this matter.

REFERENCE NOTES

Section 1

Akiskal, H.S., M.K. Khani and A. Scott-Strauss. 1979. Cyclothymic temperamental disorders. *Psychiatric Clinics of North America* 2:527-554.
Angst, J. and P. Grof. 1976. The Course of Monopolar Depressions and Bipolar Psychosis. In A. Vialleneuve, ed., *Lithium in Psychiatry: A Symposium*. Quebec: Les Presses de L'Universite Laval.
Birmaher, B., R.E. Dahl, N.D. Ryan, et al. 1992. The dexamethasone suppression test in adolescent outpatients with major depressive disorder. *American Journal of Psychiatry* 149:1040-1045.
Boyd, J.H. and M. Weissman. 1981. Epidemiology of affective disorders. *Archives of General Psychiatry* 38:1039-1046.
Brown, G.W. and T.O. Harris. 1978. *Social Origins of Depression: A Study of Psychiatric Disorders in Women*. London: Tavistock.
Cooper, J.E., R.E. Kendell, B.J. Gurland, et al. 1972. *Psychiatric Diagnosis in New York and London: A Comparative Study of Mental Hospital Admissions*. Maudsley Monograph No. 20. London: Oxford University Press.
Dubovsky, S.L. and R.D. Franks. 1983. Intracellular calcium ions in affective disorders: a review and an hypothesis. *Biological Psychiatry* 18:781-797.
Egeland, J.A. 1983. Bipolarity: the iceberg of affective disorders? *Comprehensive Psychiatry* 24:337-344.
Egeland, J.A., et al. 1987. Reliability and relationship of various ages of onset criteria for major affective disorder. *Journal of Affective Disorders* 12:159-165.
Ezquiaga, E., J.L.A. Gutierrez and A.G. Lopez. 1987. Psychosocial factors and episode number in depression. *Journal of Affective Disorders* 12:135-138.
Georgotas, A. and R. Cancero, eds. 1988. *Depression and Mania*. New York: Elsevier.

Gibbs, J.T. 1986. Assessment of depression in urban adolescent fe-males:implications for early intervention strategies. *American Journal of Social Psychiatry* 6:50-56.

Glassner, B., C.V. Haldipur and J. Dessauersmith. 1979. Role loss and working-class manic depression. *Journal of Nervous and Mental Disease* 167: 530-541.

Goodwin, F.K. and W.E. Bunny, Jr. 1971. Depressions following reserpine: a reevaluation. *Seminars in Psychiatry* 3:435-448.

Goodwin, F.K. and K.R. Jamison. 1990. *Manic-Depressive Illness.* New York: Oxford University Press.

Hill, M.A. 1992. Light, circadian rhythms and mood disorders: a review. *Annals of Clinical Psychiatry* 4:131-146.

Himmelhoch, J.M., D. Mulla, J.F. Neil, et al. 1976. Incidence and significance of mixed affective states in a bipolar population. *Archives of General Psychiatry* 33:1062-1066.

Keller, M.B. and L.A. Baker. 1992. The clinical course of panic disorder and depression. *Journal of Clinical Psychiatry* 53(3, Suppl):5-8.

Keller, M.B., P.W. Lavori, et al. 1983. "Double depression": two-year follow-up. *American Journal of Psychiatry* 140:689-694.

Klein, D.F., R. Gittleman, F. Quitkin, et al. 1981. *Diagnosis and Drug Treatment of Psychiatric Disorders: Adults and Children.* 2nd Ed. Baltimore: Williams & Wilkins.

Klein, D.N., E.B. Taylor, K. Harding, et al. 1988. Double depression and episodic major depression: demographic, clinical, familial, personality and socioenvironmental characteristics and short-term outcome. *American Journal of Psychiatry* 145:1226-1231.

Loudon, J.B., et al. 1977. A study of the symptomatology and course of manic illness. *Psychological Medicine* 723-729.

Markowitz, J.C., M.E. Moran, J.H. Kocsis, et al. 1992. Prevalence and comorbidity of dysthymic disorders among psychiatric outpatients. *Journal of Affective Disorders* 24:63-71.

Paykel, E.S., ed. 1982. *Handbook of Affective Disorders.* New York: Guilford Press, 1982.

Perris, C. 1968. The course of depressive psychosis. *Acta Psychiatrica Scandinavica* 44:238-248.

Post, R.M. 1992. Transduction of psychosocial stress into neurobiology of recurrent affective disorder. *American Journal of Psychiatry* 149:999-1010.

Raskin, A., T.H. Crook and K.D. Herman. 1975. Psychiatric history and symptom differences in black and white depressed patients. *Journal of Consulting and Clinical Psychology* 43:73-80.

Regier, D.A., J.H. Boyd, J.D. Burke, Jr., et al. 1988. One-month prevalence of mental disorders in the United States: based on five epidemiologic catchment area sites. *Archives of General Psychiatry* 45:977-986.

Samson, J.A., S.M. Mirin, S.T. Hauser, et al. 1992. Learned helplessness and urinary MHPG levels in unipolar depression. *American Journal of Psychiatry* 149:806-809.

Simpson, S.G. and J.R. DePaulo. 1991. Fluoxetine treatment of Bipolar II depression. *Journal of Clinical Psychopharmacology* 11:52-54.

Styron, W. 1990. *Darkness Visible: A Memoir of Madness*. New York: Random House.

Wehr, T.A., D.A. Sack and N.E. Rosenthal. 1987. Sleep reduction as a final common pathway in the genesis of mania. *American Journal of Psychiatry* 144:201-204.

Weissman, M.M. and J.K. Meyers. 1978. Affective disorders in a U.S. urban community. *Archives of General Psychiatry* 35:1304-1311.

Weissman, M.M. and J.K. Meyers. 1978. Rates and risks of depressive symptoms in a United States urban community. *Acta Psychiatrica Scandinavica* 57:219-231.

Weissman, M.M. and G.L. Klerman. 1977. Sex differences in the epidemiology of depression. *Archives of General Psychiatry* 34:98-111.

Winokur, G., P.J. Clayton and T. Reich. 1969. *Manic Depressive Illness*. St. Louis: C.V. Mosby Co.

Wright, J.H. and M.E. Thase. 1992. Cognitive and biological therapies: a synthesis. *Psychiatric Annals* 22:451-458.

Zisook, S. 1988. Cyclic 48-hour unipolar depression. *Journal of Nervous and Mental Disease* 176:53-56.

Section 2

Akiskal, H.S. 1985. The Clinical Management of Affective Disorders. In J.O. Cavenar, ed., *Psychiatry*. Vol. 1. Philadelphia: Lippincott.

Anton, R.F., Jr. and E.A. Burch. 1990. Amoxapine versus amitriptyline combined with perphenazine in the treatment of psychotic depression. *American Journal of Psychiatry* 147:1203-1208.

Apseloff, G., K.D. Wilner, D.A. von Deutsch, et al. 1992. Sertraline does not alter steady-state concentrations or renal clearance of lithium in healthy volunteers. *Journal of Clinical Pharmacology* 32:643-646.

Avery, D. and G. Winokur. 1976. Mortality in depressed patients treated with electroconvulsive therapy and antidepressants. *Archives of General Psychiatry* 133:1029-1037.

Ballentine, H.T., B.S. Levy, T.F. Dagi, et al. 1977. Cingulotomy for Psychiatric Illness: Report of 13 years' Experience. In W.H. Sweet, S. Obrador and J.G. Martin-Rodriguez, eds., *Neurosurgical Treatment in Psychiatry, Pain and Epilepsy*. Baltimore: University Park Press.

Ballinger, J.C. and R.M. Post. 1978. Kindling as a model for alcohol withdrawal syndromes. *British Journal of Psychiatry* 133:1-14.

Balogh, S. 1992. Treatment of fluoxetine-induced anorgasmia with amantadine. *Journal of Clinical Psychiatry* 53:212-213.

Bauer, M.S. and P.C. Whybrow. 1990. Rapid cycling bipolar affective disorder, II: treatment of refractory rapid cycling with high-dose levothyroxine: a preliminary study. *Archives of General Psychiatry* 47:435-440.

Baxter, L.R., Jr., et al. 1985. Cerebral metabolic rates for glucose in mood disorders. *Archives of General Psychiatry* 42:441-447

Beck, A.T., J. Rush, B. Shaw, et al. 1979. *Cognitive Therapy of Depression.* New York: Guilford Press.

Bezchlibnyk-Butler, K.Z. and J.J. Jeffries. 1991. *Clinical Handbook of Psychotropic Drugs* (3rd Ed.). Toronto: Hogrefe & Huber.

Biederman, J. et al. 1979. Combination of lithium carbonate and haloperidol in schizoaffective disorder: a controlled study. *Archives of General Psychiatry* 36:327-333.

Bixler, E.O., A. Kales, et al. 1991. Next-day memory impairment with triazolam use. *The Lancet* 1:827-831.

Blay, S.L., M.P.T. Ferrez and H.M. Cali. 1982. Lithium-induced male sexual impairment: two case reports. *Journal of Clinical Psychiatry* 43:497-498.

Bowe, R.C., P. Grof and E. Grof. 1991. Less frequent lithium administration and lower urine volume. *American Journal of Psychiatry* 148:189-192.

Buff, D., et al. 1991. Dysrhythmia associated with fluoxetine in an elderly patient with cardiac disease. *Journal of Clinical Psychiatry* 52:174-176.

Burke, W.J., et al. 1987. The safety of ECT in geriatric psychiatry. *Journal of the American Geriatric Society* 35:516-521.

Burns, C.M. and G.W. Stuart. 1991. Nursing care in electroconvulsive therapy. *Psychiatric Clinics of North America* 14:971-984.

Burns, D.D. and A.H. Auerbach. 1992. Does homework compliance enhance recovery from depression? *Psychiatric Annals* 22:464-469.

Calabrese, J.R. and G.A. Delucchi. 1990. Spectrum of efficacy of valproate in 55 patients with rapid-cycling bipolar disorder. *American Journal of Psychiatry* 147:431-434.

Causemann, B. and B. Muller-Oerlinghausen. 1988. Does lithium reduce prevent suicides and suicide attempts? In N. Birch, ed., *Lithium: Inorganic Pharmacology and Psychiatric Use.* Oxford: IRL Press.

Chambers, C.A., et al. 1982. The effect of digoxin on the response to lithium therapy in mania. *Psychological Medicine* 12:57-60.

Chou, J.C.Y. 1991. Recent advances in the treatment of acute mania. *Journal of Clinical Psychopharmacology* 11:3-21.

Clary, C. and E. Schweitzer. 1987. Treatment of MAOI hypertensive crisis with sublingual nifedipine. *Journal of Clinical Psychiatry* 48:249-250.

Cole, J.O. and J.A. Bodkin. 1990. Antidepressant drug side effects. *Journal of Clinical Psychiatry* 51(1, Suppl.):21-26.

Consensus Development Panel. 1985. Mood disorders: pharmacological prevention of recurrences. *American Journal of Psychiatry* 142:469-475.

Coppen, A., H. Standish-Barry, J. Bailey, et al. 1991. Does lithium reduce the mortality of recurrent mood disorders? *Journal of Affective Disorders* 23:1-7.

Damluji, N.F. and J.M. Ferguson. 1988. Paradoxical worsening of depressive symptomatology caused by antidepressants. *Journal of Clinical Psychopharmacology* 8:347-349.

Decina, P., E.B. Guthrie, et al. 1987. Continuation ECT in the management of relapses of major affective episodes. *Acta Psychiatrica Scandinavica* 75:559-562.

Detre, T.P. and H.G. Jarecki. 1971. *Modern Psychiatric Treatment*. Philadelphia: Lippincott.

Devanand, D.P. et al. 1991. Absence of cognitive impairment after more than 100 lifetime ECT treatments. *American Journal of Psychiatry* 148:929-932.

Dunner, D.L. and R.R. Fieve. 1974. Clinical factors in lithium carbonate prophylaxis failure. *Archives of General Psychiatry* 30:229-233.

Eisenberg, L. 1992. Treating depression and anxiety in primary care: closing the gap between knowledge and practice. *New England Journal of Medicine* 326:1080-1084.

Evans, M. and P. Marwick. 1990. Fluvoxamine and lithium: an unusual interaction. *British Journal of Psychiatry* 156:286.??Everett, H.C. 1975. The use of bethanechol chloride with tricyclic antidepressants. *American Journal of Psychiatry* 132:1202-1204.

Extein, I. and M.S. Gold. 1986. Psychiatric applications of thyroid tests. *Journal of Clinical Psychiatry* 47(1, Suppl.):13-16.

Fava, G.A. and R. Kellner. 1991. Prodromal symptoms in affective disorders. *American Journal of Psychiatry* 148:823-830.

Fernstrom, M., L.H. Epstein, et al. 1985. Resting metabolic rate is reduced in patients treated with antidepressants. *Biological Psychiatry* 20:688-692.

Fitton, A., D. Faulds and K.L. Goa. 1992. Moclobemide: a review of its pharmacological properties and therapeutic use in depressive illness. *Drugs* 43:561-596.

Frank, E. D.J. Kupfer, J.M. Perel, et al. 1990. Three year outcomes for maintenance therapies for recurrent depressions. *Archives of General Psychiatry* 47:1093-1099.

Freeman, C.P.L. and R.E. Kendell. 1986. Patients' experiences of and attitudes to electroconvulsive therapy. *Archives of the New York Academy of Sciences* 462: 341-352.

Fulder, S.J. 1981. Ginseng and the hypothalamic-pituitary control of stress. *American Journal of Chinese Medicine* 9:112-118.

Gardner, E.A. and J.A. Johnston. 1985. Bupropion: an antidepressant without sexual pathophysiological action. *Journal of Clinical Psychopharmacology* 5:24-29.

Garve, M., R.J. DeRubeis, et al. 1991. Response of depression to very high plasma levels of imipramine plus desipramine. *Biological Psychiatry* 30:57-62.

Gold, M.S. and H.R. Pearsall. 1983. Depression and hypothyroidism. *Journal of the American Medical Association* 250:2470-2471.

Greist, J.H., M.H. Klein, et al. 1979. Running as treatment for depression. *Comprehensive Psychiatry* 20:41-54.

Gross, M.D. 1982. Reversal by bethanechol of sexual dysfunction caused by anticholinergic antidepressants. *American Journal of Psychiatry* 139:1193-1194.

Guscott, R. and P. Grof. 1991. The clinical meaning of refractory depression: a review for the clinician. *American Journal of Psychiatry* 148:695-707.

Harto-Truax, N., et al. 1983. Effects of bupropion on body weight. *Journal of Clinical Psychiatry* 44(5, Suppl.):183-186.

Harrison, W.M., P.J. McGrath, et al. 1989. MAOIs and hypertensive crises: the role of OTC drugs. *Journal of Clinical Psychiatry* 50:64-65.

Hayes, S.G. 1989. Long-term use of valproate in primary psychiatric disorders. *Journal of Clinical Psychiatry* 50:35-39.

Heninger, G.R., D.S. Charney and D.E. Sternberg. 1983. Lithium carbonate augmentation of antidepressant treatment: an effective prescription for treatment-refractory depression. *Archives of General Psychiatry* 40:1335-1342

Himmelhoch, J.M., T. Detre, et al. 1972. Treatment of previously intractable depressions with tranylcypromine and lithium. *Journal of Nervous and Mental Disease* 155:216-220.

Jacobsen, F.M. 1991. Possible augmentation of antidepressant response by buspirone. *Journal of Clinical Psychiatry* 52:217-220.

Jacobsen, F.M. 1992. Fluoxetine-induced sexual dysfunction and an open trial of yohimbine. *Journal of Clinical Psychiatry* 53:119-122.

Jefferson, J.W. 1992. Treatment of depressed patients who have become nontolerant to antidepressant medication because of cardiovascular side effects. *Journal of Clinical Psychiatry Monograph* 10(1):66-71.

Kantor, S.J. 1990. Depression: When is psychotherapy not enough? *Psychiatric Clinics of North America* 13:241-254.

Keck, P.E., S.L. McElroy, A. Vuckovic, et al. 1992. Combined valproate and carbamazepine treatment of bipolar disorder. *Journal of Neuropsychiatry and Clinical Neurosciences* 4:319-322.

Keller, M.B., P.W. Lavori, et al. 1992. Subsyndromal symptoms in bipolar disorder: A comparison of standard and low serum levels of lithium. *Archives of General Psychiatry* 49:371-376.

Klerman, G.L., M.M. Weissman, et al. 1984. *Interpersonal Psychotherapy of Depression*. New York: Basic Books.

Kocsis, J.H., A.J. Frances, et al. 1988. Imipramine treatment for chronic depression. *Archives of General Psychiatry* 45:253-257.

Kramer, B.A. 1985. The use of ECT in California, 1977-1983. *American Journal of Psychiatry* 142:1190-1192.

Kramer, B.A. 1986. Maintenance ECT: a survey of practice. *Convulsive Therapies* 3:260-268.Mayo, J.A. 1979. Marital therapy with manic-depressive patients treated with lithium. *Comprehensive Psychiatry* 20:419-426.

Macleod, A.D. 1991. Paradoxical responses to antidepressant medications. *Annals of Clinical Psychiatry* 3:239-242.

Miklowitz, D.J. M.J. Goldstein, et al. 1988. Family factors and the corse of bipolar affective disorder. *Archives of General Psychiatry* 45:225-231.

Mitchell, P. and M.J. Cullen. 1991. Valproate for rapid-cycling unipolar affective disorder. *Journal of Nervous and Mental Disease* 179:503-504.

Monroe, R.R. 1991. Maintenance electroconvulsive therapy. *Psychiatric Clinics of North America* 14:947-960.

Montgomery, S.A., H. Dufour, et al. 1988. The prophylactic efficacy of fluoxetine in unipolar depression. *British Journal of Psychiatry* 153(9, Suppl.):69-76.

Müller-Oerlinghausen, B.B. Ahrens, et al. 1991. Reduced mortality of manic-depressive patients in long-term lithium treatment: an international collaborative study by IGSLI. *Psychiatry Research* 36:329-331.

Nelson, J.C., C.M. Mazure and M.B. Bowers, Jr. 1991. A preliminary open study of the combination of fluoxetine and desipramine for rapid treatment of major depression. *Archives of General Psychiatry* 48:303-307.

Nora, J.J., H.A. Nora and W.H. Toew. 1974. Lithium, Ebstein's anomaly and other congenital heart defects. *The Lancet* 2:594-595.

Penney, J.F., et al. 1990. Concurrent and close temporal administration of lithium and ECT. *Convulsive Therapies* 6:139-145.

Perry, P.J., et al. 1984. Treatment of unipolar depression accompanied by delusions. *Journal of Affective Disorders* 4:195-200.

Post, R.M. 1988. Time course of clinical effects of carbamazepine: implications for mechanism of action. *Journal of Clinical Psychiatry* 49(4, Suppl.):35-46.

Post, R.M. 1990. Alternatives to Lithium for Bipolar Affective Illness. In *Review of Psychiatry*, Vol 9. Washington, DC: American Psychiatric Press.

Post, R.M. 1990. Non-lithium treatment for bipolar disorder. *Journal of Clinical Psychiatry* 51(8, Suppl.):9-16.

Price, L.H., D.S. Charney and G.R. Heninger. 1984. Three cases of manic symptoms following yohimbine administration. *American Journal of Psychiatry* 141:1267-1268.

Prien, R.F., D.J. Kupfer, P.A. Mansky, et al. 1984. Drug therapy in the prevention of recurrences of unipolar and bipolar affective disorders. *Archives of General Psychiatry* 41:1096-1104.

Quitkin, F.M., J. Kane, A. Rifkin, et al. 1981. Prophylactic lithium carbonate with and without imipramine for Bipolar I patients: a double-blind study. *Archives of General Psychiatry* 38:902-907.

Roose, S.P., A.H. Glassman, B.T. Walsh, et al. 1983. Depression, delusions and suicide. *American Journal of Psychiatry* 140:1159-1162.

Roose, S.P., G.W. Dalack, et al. Cardiovascular effects of Bupropion in depressed patients with heart disease. *American Journal of Psychiatry* 148:512-516.

Rosenbaum, A.H. R.G. Niven, N.P. Hanson, et al. 1977. Tardive dyskinesia: relationship with primary affective disorder. *Diseases of the Nervous System* 38: 423-427.

Rothchild, A. and C. Locke. 1991. Reexposure to fluoxetine after serious suicide attempts by three patients: the role of akathisia. *Journal of Clinical Psychiatry* 52:491-493.

Sachdev, P., J.J. Smith and J. Matheson. 1988. Psychosurgery for bipolar affective disorder. *British Journal of Psychiatry* 153:576.

Sackeim, H.A. 1991. The Cognitive Effects of Electroconvulsive Therapy. In I.J. Thal, W.H. Moos and E. Gamzu, eds., *Cognitive Disorders: Pathophysiology and Treatment.* New York: Marcel Dekker.

Schou, M. 1979. Artistic productivity and lithium prophylaxis in manic depressive illness. *British Journal of Psychiatry* 135:97-103.

Schou, M. 1976. What happened to the lithium babies? a follow-up study of children born without malformations. *Acta Psychiatrica Scandinavica* 54:193-197.

Schou, M., et al. 1977. Lithium treatment regimen and renal water handling: the significance of dosage pattern and tablet type examined through comparison of results from two clinics with different treatment regimens. *Psychopharmacology* 77:387-390.

Scott, A.I.F., et al. 1991. Electroconvulsive therapy and brain damage. *The Lancet* 2:264.

Secunda, S.K., A. Swann, M.M. Katz, et al. 1987. Diagnosis and treatment of mixed mania. *American Journal of Psychiatry* 144:96-98.

Shapira, B., A. Calev and B. Lerer. 1991. Optimal use of electroconvulsive therapy: choosing a treatment schedule. *Psychiatric Clinics of North America* 14:935-946.

Shulman, K.I. 1989. Dietary restriction, tyramine, and the use of monoamine oxidase inhibitors. *Journal of Clinical Psychopharmacology* 9:397-401.

Siegel, R.K. 1979. Ginseng abuse syndrome: problems with the panacea. *Journal of the American Medical Association* 241:1614-1615.

Simons, A.D., G.E. Murphy and J.L. Levine. 1986. Relapse after treatment with cognitive therapy and/or pharmacotherapy: results after one year. *Archives of General Psychiatry* 43:43-48.

Small, J.G., V. Milstein, M.H. Klapper, et al. 1986. Electroconvulsive therapy in the treatment of manic episodes. *Annals of the New York Academy of Sciences* 462:37-49.

Sovner, R. 1984. Treatment of tricyclic antidepressant-induced orgasmic inhibition with cyproheptadine. *Journal of Clinical Psychopharmacology* 4:169.

Spiker, D.G., et al. 1985. Pharmacological treatment of delusional depression. American Journal of Psychiatry 142:430-436.

Squires, L.R., et al. 1983. Electroconvulsive therapy and complaints of memory dysfunction: a prospective three-year follow-up study. *British Journal of Psychiatry* 142:1-8.

Squires, L.R. 1986. Memory functions affected by electroconvulsive therapy. *Annals of the New York Academy of Sciences* 462:307-314.

Sullivan, E.A. and K.I. Schulman. 1984. Diet and monoamine oxidase inhibition: A reexamination. *Canadian Journal of Psychiatry* 29:707-711.

Teicher, M.H., C. Glad and J.O. Cole. 1990. Emergence of intense suicidal preoccupation during fluoxetine treatment. *American Journal of Psychiatry* 147:207-210.

Thompson, J.W., Jr., M.R. Ware and R.K. Blashfield. 1990. Psychotropic medication and priapism: a comprehensive review. *Journal of Clinical Psychiatry* 51:430-433.

Thase, M.E., A.D. Simons, et al. 1992. Relapse after cognitive behavior therapy for depression: potential implications for longer courses of treatment. *American Journal of Psychiatry* 149:1046-1052.

Wehr, T.A. 1992. Improvement of depression and triggering of mania by sleep deprivation. *Journal of the American Medical Association* 267:548-551.

Wehr, T.A. and F.K. Goodwin. 1987. Can antidepressants cause mania and worsen the course of affective illness? *American Journal of Psychiatry* 144:1403-1411.

Wehr, T.A., D.A. Sack, N.E. Rosenthal, et al. 1988. Rapid cycling affective disorder: contributing factors and treatment response in 51 patients. *American Journal of Psychiatry* 145:179-184.

Weisler, R.H. 1992. Treatment strategies for lithium-resistant bipolar depression. *Journal of Clinical Psychiatry* 10(1):27-32.

Wright, R., G. Galloway, L. Kim, et al. 1985. Bupropion in the long-term treatment of cyclic mood disorders: mood stabilizing effects. *Journal of Clinical Psychiatry* 46:22-25.

Section 3

Allen, R.E. and F.N. Pitts, Jr. 1978. ECT for depressed patients with lupus erythematosus. *American Journal of Psychiatry* 135:367-368.

Angrist, B., M. d'Hollosy, M. Sanfilipo, et al. 1992. Central nervous system stimulants as symptomatic treatment for AIDS-related neuropsychiatric impairment. *Journal of Clinical Psychopharmacology* 12:268-272.

Beck, A.T., R.A. Steer, M. Kovacs, et al. 1985. Hopelessness and eventual suicide: A 10-year prospective study of patients hospitalized with suicidal ideation. *American Journal of Psychiatry* 142:559-563.

Blazer, D., D.C. Hughes and K. George. 1987. The epidemiology of depression in an elderly community population. *The Gerontologist* 27:281-287.

Bruera, E. 1984. Use of methylphenidate as an adjuvant to narcotic analgesics in patients with advanced cancer. *Journal of Pain and Symptom Management* 4:3.

Burns, B.J., et al. 1988. Mental disorders among nursing home patients: preliminary findings from the national nursing home survey pretest. *International Journal of Geriatric Psychiatry* 3:27-35.

Butler, S. T., Chalder, M. Ron, et al. 1991. Cognitive behavior therapy in chronic fatigue syndrome. *Journal of Neurology, Neurosurgery and Psychiatry* 54:153-158.

Carlson, G.A., Y.B. Davenport and K. Jamison. 1977. A comparison of outcome in adolescent and late-onset bipolar manic-depressive illness. *American Journal of Psychiatry* 134:919-922.

Carlson, G.A. and M. Strober. 1978. Affective disorder in adolescence: issues in misdiagnosis. *Journal of Clinical Psychiatry* 39:59-66.

Chandraiah, S., J.L. Levenson and J.B. Collins. 1991. Sexual dysfunction, social maladjustment and psychiatric disorders in women seeking treatment in a premenstrual syndrome clinic. *International Journal of Psychiatry in Medicine* 21:189-204.

Clark, A.F. and K. Davidson. 1987. Mania following head injury: a report of two cases and a review of the literature. *British Journal of Psychiatry* 150:841-844.

Clayton, P.J. 1990. Bereavement and depression. *Journal of Clinical Psychiatry* 50 (7 Suppl.):34-38.

Cohen, C.K., R. Shrivastava, J. Mendels, et al. 1990. Double-blind, multicenter comparisons of sertraline and amitriptyline in elderly depressed patients. *Journal of Clinical Psychiatry* 51 (12 Suppl. B):28-33.

Currier, M.B., G.B. Murray and C.C. Welch. 1992. Electroconvulsive therapy for post-stroke depressed geriatric patients. *Journal of Neuropsychiatry and Clinical Neurosciences* 4:140-144.

Dalack, G.W. and S.P. Roose. 1990. Perspectives on the relationship between cardiovascular disease and affective disorder. *Journal of Clinical Psychiatry* 51 (7 Suppl.):4-9.

Deeny, M., R. Hawthorn and D. McKay-Hart. 1991. Low dose danazol in the treatment of the premenstrual syndrome. *Postgraduate Medical Journal* 67:450-4.

Fawcett, J., W. Scheftner, D. Clark, et al. 1987. Clinical predictors of suicide in patients with major affective disorders: a controlled prospective study. *American Journal of Psychiatry* 144:35-40.

Fedoroff, J.P. and R.G. Robinson. 1989. Tricyclic antidepressants in the treatment of poststroke depression. *Journal of Clinical Psychiatry* 50(7, Suppl.): 18-23.

Gitlin, M.J. and R.O. Pasnau. 1988. Psychiatric syndromes linked to reproductive function in women: a review of current knowledge. *American Journal of Psychiatry* 146:1414-1422.Glick, I.O. 1974. *The First Year of Bereavement*. New York: John Wiley & Sons.

Goetz, C.G., C.M. Tanner and H.L. Klawans. 1984. Bupropion in Parkinson's disease. *Neurology* 34:1092-1094.

Hekimian, L.J. and S. Gershon. 1986. Characteristics of drug abusers admitted to a psychiatric hospital. *Journal of the American Medical Association* 205:125-130.

Henderson, R. Kurlan, J.M. Kersun, et al. 1992. Preliminary examination of the comorbidity of anxiety and depression in Parkinson's disease. *Journal of Neuropsychiatry* 4:357-264.

Jenike, M.A. 1985. MAO inhibitors as treatment for depressed patients with primary degenerative dementia (Alzheimer's disease). *American Journal of Psychiatry* 142:763-764.

Juel-Nielsen, N. and T. Videbech. 1970. A twin study of suicide. *Acta Psychiatrica Scandinavica* 19:307-310.

Kaufman, J. 1991. Depressive disorders in maltreated children. *Journal of the American Academy of Child and Adolescent Psychiatry* 2:257-265.

Kellerman, A.L., F.P. Rivara, G. Somes, et al. 1992. Suicide in the home in relation to gun ownership. *New England Journal of medicine.* 327:467-472.

Kendell, R.E., S. Wainwright, A. Hailey, et al. 1976. Influence of childbirth on psychiatric morbidity. *Psychological Medicine* 6:297-302.

Kendell, R.E., J.C. Chalmers and C. Platz. 1987. Epidemiology of puerperal psychoses. *British Journal of Psychiatry* 150:662-673.

Kestenbaum, C.J. 1979. Children at risk for manic-depressive illness: possible predictors. *American Journal of Psychiatry* 136:1206-1208.

Levav, I., et al. An epidemiologic study of mortality among bereaved parents. *New England Journal of Medicine,* 319:457-461.

Loebel, J.P., J.S. Loebel, S.R. Dager, et al. 1991. Anticipation of nursing home placement may be a precipitant of suicide among the elderly. *Journal of the American Geriatrics Society* 39:407-409.

Lovett, L.M. and D.M. Shaw. 1987. Outcome in bipolar affective disorder after stereotactic tractotomy. *British Journal of Psychiatry* 151:113-116.

Maddison, D. and D. Viola. 1968. The health of widows in the year following bereavement. *Journal of Psychosomatic Research* 12:297-306.

Malzberg, B. 1937. Mortality among patients with involution melancholia. *American Journal of Psychiatry* 93:1231-1238.

Massie, M.J. and J.C. Holland. 1990. Depression and the cancer patient. *Journal of Clinical Psychiatry* 51(7, Suppl.):12-17.

Mayeux, R. 1990. Depression in the patient with Parkinson's disease. *Journal of Clinical Psychiatry* 51(7 Suppl.):20-23.

Meehan, P.J., L.E. Saltzman and R.W. Sattin. 1991. Suicides among older United States residents: epidemiologic characteristics and trends. *American Journal of Public Health* 81:1198-1200.

Minden, S.L., J. Orav. and J.J. Schildkraut. 1988. Hypomanic reactions to ACTH and prednisone treatment for multiple sclerosis. *Neurology* 38:1631-1634.

Morse, C.A., L. Dennerstein. E. Farrell, et al. 1991. A comparison of hormone therapy, coping skills training and relaxation for the relief of premenstrual syndrome. *Journal of Behavioral Medicine* 14:469-89.

NIH Consensus Development Panel of Depression in Late Life. 1992. Diagnosis and treatment of depression in late life. *Journal of the American Medical Association* 268:1018-1024.

O'Connell, R.A., J.A. Mayo, L. Flatlow, et al. 1991. Outcome of bipolar disorder on long-term treatment with lithium. *British Journal of Psychiatry* 159:123-129.

Osterweiss, M., et al., eds. 1984. *Bereavement: Reactions, Consequences and Care*. Washington, DC: National Academy Press, 1984.

Pomara, N. and S. Gershon. 1984. Treatment-resistant depression in an elderly patient with pancreatic carcinoma: case report. *Journal of Clinical Psychiatry* 439-440.

Reiger, D.A., M.E. Farmer, D.S. Rae, et al. 1990. Comorbidity of mental disorders with alcohol and other drug abuse. *Journal of the American Medical Association* 264:2511-2518.

Reynolds, C.F., C.C. Hoch, D.J. Kupfer, et al. 1988. Bedside differentiation of depressive pseudodementia from dementia. *American Journal of Psychiatry* 145: 1099-1103.

Robinson, R.G,, P.L.P. Morris and J.L. Fedoroff. 1990. Depression and cerebrovascular disease. *Journal of Clinical Psychiatry* 51(7, Suppl.):26-31.

Rovner, B.W., P.S. German, L.J. Brant, et al. 1991. Depression and mortality in nursing homes. *Journal of the American Medical Association* 265:993-996.

Runeson, B. 1989. Mental disorders in youth suicides: DSM-III-R Axes I and II. *Acta Psychiatrica Scandinavica* 79:490-497.

Shaffer, R.B., R.M. Herndon and R.A. Rudick. 1985. Treatment of pathological laughing and weeping with amitriptyline. *New England Journal of Medicine* 312: 1480-1482.

Shneidman, E.S. 1975. Suicide. In A.M. Friedman, B.J. Kaplan, et al., eds., *Comprehensive Textbook of Psychiatry*. 2nd Ed., Vol. 2. Baltimore: Williams & Wilkins.

Shopsin, B. and S. Gershon. 1975. Cogwheel rigidity related to lithium maintenance. *American Journal of Psychiatry* 132:536-538.

Siegal, F.P. 1978. Lithium for steroid-induced psychosis. *New England Journal of Medicine* 299:155-156.Spitz, R.A. and K.M. Wolf. 1946. Anaclitic depression. *Psychoanalytic Study of the Child* 2:313-342.

Starkstein, S.E., H.S. Mayberg, M.L. Berthier, et al. 1990. Mania after brain injury: neuroradiological and metabolic findings. *Annals of Neurology* 27: 652-659.

Warneke, L. 1990. Psychostimulants in psychiatry. *Canadian Journal of Psychiatry* 35:3-9.

Weiner, M.F., et al. 1991. Experiences with depression in a dementia clinic. *Journal of Clinical Psychiatry* 52:234-238.

Weissman, M.M., G.D. Gammon, K. John, et al. 1987. Children of depressed parents: increased psychopathology and early onset of major depression. *Archives of General Psychiatry* 44:847-853.

Young, M., et al. 1963. Mortality of widowers. *The Lancet* 2:454.

Young, R.C. 1992. Geriatric mania. *Clinics in Geriatric Medicine* 8:387-399.

SUGGESTED READINGS

The A.A. Member—Medications and Other Drugs. 1984. New York: Alcoholics Anonymous World Service. (Available from: A.A., Box 459, Grand Central Station, New York, NY 10163).

Andreasen, N. 1985. *The Broken Brain: The Biological Revolution in Psychiatry.* New York: Harper and Row.

Burns, D.D. 1980. *Feeling Good: The New Mood Therapy.* New York: Signet.

DePaulo, J.R. and K.R. Ablow. 1989. *How to Cope with Depression: A Complete Guide for You and Your Family.* New York: Fawcett Crest.

Lewinsohn, P.M., R.F. Munoz, M.A. Youngren and A.M. Zeiss. 1986. *Control Your Depression.* New York: Prentice Hall.

Papolos, D. and J. Papolos. 1992. *Overcoming Depression* (Revised Edition). 1992. New York: HarperCollins.

Shimberg, E.F., 1991. *Depression: What Families Should Know.* New York: Ballantine Books.

Wender, P.H. and D.F. Klein. 1981. *Mind, Mood, and Medicine: A Guide to the New Biopsychiatry.* New York: New American Library.

The Goldberg Mood Scales

On the next pages you will find copies of the Goldberg Mania and Depression Scales. These self-administered questionnaires are designed to measure the severity of manic and depressive thinking and behavior.

If you suspect that you may have a mood disorder, these scales may help you decide whether you should schedule a psychiatric evaluation. The scales are not designed diagnose any psychiatric disorder, they just measure the severity of depressive and manic symptoms. A score of 15 or more on the depression scale, or a score of 20 or more on the mania scale, suggests the need for a psychiatric evaluation. The actual diagnosis of a mood disorder can only be made after a complete medical and psychiatric evaluation.

If you are already being treated for a mood disorder you may find these scales to be a useful way to keep track of your progress. Photocopy the scales and complete them once a week to measure the severity of your mood symptoms.

APPENDIX 1
The Goldberg Mania Scale

Name _____   Date _____

The items below refer to how you have felt and behaved <u>during the past week</u>.
For each statement, indicate the extent to which it is true by circling one of
the numbers according to this scale:

0 = Not at all   1 = Just a little 2 = Somewhat   3 = Moderately   4 = Quite a lot   5 = Very much

1. My mind has never been sharper.	0 1 2 3 4 5
2. I need less sleep than usual.	0 1 2 3 4 5
3. I have so many plans that it's hard for me to work.	0 1 2 3 4 5
4. I feel a pressure to talk and talk.	0 1 2 3 4 5
5. I have been particularly happy.	0 1 2 3 4 5
6. I have been more active than usual.	0 1 2 3 4 5
7. I talk so fast that people can't keep up with me.	0 1 2 3 4 5
8. I have more new ideas than I can handle.	0 1 2 3 4 5
9. I have been irritable.	0 1 2 3 4 5
10. It's easy for me to think of jokes and funny stories.	0 1 2 3 4 5
11. I have been feeling like "the life of the party."	0 1 2 3 4 5
12. I have been full of energy.	0 1 2 3 4 5
13. I have been thinking about sex.	0 1 2 3 4 5
14. I have been particularly playful.	0 1 2 3 4 5
15. I have special plans for the world.	0 1 2 3 4 5
16. I have been spending too much money.	0 1 2 3 4 5
17. My attention keeps jumping from one idea to another.	0 1 2 3 4 5
18. I find it hard to slow down and stay in one place	0 1 2 3 4 5

APPENDIX 2
The Goldberg Depression Scale

Name _____   Date _____

The items below refer to how you have felt and behaved <u>during the past week</u>. For each statement, indicate the extent to which it is true by circling one of the numbers according to this scale:

0 = Not at all   1 = Just a little   2 = Somewhat   3 = Moderately   4 = Quite a lot   5 = Very much

1. I do things slowly.	0 1 2 3 4 5
2. My future seems hopeless.	0 1 2 3 4 5
3. It is hard for me to concentrate on reading.	0 1 2 3 4 5
4. The pleasure and joy has gone out of my life.	0 1 2 3 4 5
5. I have difficulty making decisions.	0 1 2 3 4 5
6. I've lost interest in things that used to be important.	0 1 2 3 4 5
7. I feel sad, blue and unhappy.	0 1 2 3 4 5
8. I am agitated and keep moving around.	0 1 2 3 4 5
9. I feel fatigued.	0 1 2 3 4 5
10. It takes great effort for me to do simple things.	0 1 2 3 4 5
11. I am a guilty person who deserves punishment.	0 1 2 3 4 5
12. I feel like a failure.	0 1 2 3 4 5
13. I feel lifeless and more dead than alive.	0 1 2 3 4 5
14. My sleep is disturbed — too little, too much, broken.	0 1 2 3 4 5
15. I spend time thinking about how I might kill myself.	0 1 2 3 4 5
16. I feel trapped or caught.	0 1 2 3 4 5
17. I feel depressed even when good things happen.	0 1 2 3 4 5
18. Without trying to diet, I have lost or gained weight.	0 1 2 3 4 5

APPENDIX 3
List of Drugs used for Mood Disorders

Brand Name	Generic Name	Brand Name	Generic Name
Akineton	biperiden	Janimine	imipramine
Anafranil	clomipramine	Kemadrin	procyclidine
Artane	trihexphendyl	Klonopin	clonazepam
Asendin	amoxapine	Librium	chlordiazepoxide
Atarax	lorazepam	Lithane	lithium carbonate
Ativan	lorazepam	Lithobid	lithium carbonate
Aventyl	nortriptyline	Loxitane	loxapine
Calan	verapamil	Ludiomil	maprotoline
Centrax	prazepam	Luvox	fluvoxamine
Cibalith-S	lithium citrate	Manerix	moclobemide
Clozaril	clozapine	Marplan	isocarboxazid
Cogentin	benztropine	Mellaril	thioridazine
Dalmane	flurazepam	Miltown	meprobamate
Danocrine	danazol	Moban	molindone
Depakene	valproate (valproic acid)	Mogadon	nitrazepam
		Nardil	phenelzine
Depakote	valproate (valproic acid)	Navane	thiothixene
		Norpramin	desipramine
Desyrel	trazodone	Pamelor	nortriptyline
Dexedrine	dextroamphetamine	Parnate	tranylcypromine
Doral	quazepam	Paxil	paroxetine
Elavil	amitriptyline	Periactin	cyproheptadine
Eskalith	lithium carbonate	Prolixin	fluphenazine
Fluanxol	flupenthixol	ProSom	estazolam
Haldol	haloperidol	Prozac	fluoxetine
Isoptin	verapamil	Restoril	temazepam
Inderal	propranolol	Ritalin	methylphenidate

Brand Name	Generic Name	Brand Name	Generic Name
Rivotril	clonazepam	Tofranil	imipramine
Serax	oxazepam	Tranxene	clorazepate
Serentil	mesoridazine	Trilafon	perphenazine
Sinequan	doxepin	Valium	diazepam
Stelazine	trifluoperazine	Vistaril	hydroxyzine
Surmontil	trimipramine	Vivactil	protriptyline
Symetrel	amantadine	Wellbutrin	bupropion
Taractan	chlorprothixene	Xanax	alprazolam
Tegretol	carbamazepine	Zoloft	sertraline
Thorazine	chlorpromazine		

How To Get Help

There are support groups in almost every state in the U.S. For detailed information about how to locate a group in your city or town, the National Depressive and Manic-Depressive Association will be glad to help you.

National Depresive and Manic-Depressive Association
730 N. Franklin
Suite 501
Chicago, Illinois 60610

Their toll-free number is: 1-800-82N-DMDA.

A Note to Readers

It is expected that this book will be revised from time to time. If you have a question regarding depression or manic-depression that you would like to see answered in the next edition of this book, please submit it on the form below.

Dear Dr. Goldberg:

Please answer the following question when you revise *Questions and Answers about Depression and Its Treatment*:

_____

_____

_____

_____

Mail to:

Ivan K. Goldberg, M.D.
1346 Lexington Avenue
New York, NY 10128

Submitted by:

_____
Name

_____
Address

_____
City   State   Zip

Notes

Notes

Notes

Notes

Notes